Nordic N[...]

Articles on cross-country skiing

By Stuart Montgomery

Second edition. Copyright © Stuart Montgomery 2015.

All rights reserved. No part of this publication may be reproduced or transmitted in any form or by any means, electronic or mechanical, without permission in writing from the publisher.

Most photographs were taken by the author. The exceptions, which are acknowledged with thanks, are: 2.1 (Helen Brown), 3.1 (Mary Campbell), 5.1 & 5.8 (Clare Byrne), 5.3 & 5.6 (Kevin Hesketh), 6.5 (Geir Andre Olsen/Gunnarbu webcam), 9.1, 9.2 & 9.5 (Sue Webb).

Some of the articles in this book discuss kit and clothing, and in so doing they occasionally mention brand names. The author wants to make it clear that he is not commercially linked to any supplier.

Important: Many of the articles in this book talk about the benefits of strenuous activity. But if you have any doubts about your own health you should take medical advice before undertaking any such activity.

CONTENTS

INTRODUCTION

SECTION 1: COUNTRY LIFE

1.1 Fire at Rondvassbu Hut

1.2 Galdhøpiggen ski race

1.3 Look up! Things to see in the sky

1.4 Lillehammer Youth Hostel

1.5 Mountain transport in Høvringen

SECTION 2: SKIING WITH CHILDREN

2.1 Barnas Holmenkolldag

2.2 Skiing with children — a cautionary tale

SECTION 3: SKIING TIPS FOR BEGINNERS

3.1 Half snowplough

3.2 Going faster (by not going so slowly)

3.3 Downhill skills

SECTION 4: EQUIPMENT AND WAXING

4.1 End of season tidy-up

4.2 Choosing climbing skins

4.3 When skis ball-up

SECTION 5: TOURING IN NORWAY

5.1 Norwegian mountain huts: DNT

5.2 Troll Loipe

5.3 Rondane

5.4 Finse Hut

5.5 More about Rondane

5.6 Touring in warm weather

5.7 Dave Leaning: Lindesnes to Nordkapp

5.8 Peer Gynt Loipe

SECTION 6: GENERAL FEATURES

6.1 Skarverennet

6.2 How big is the British XC ski market?

6.3 London rollerski race

6.4 Cross-country skiing for blind people

6.5 Norway in January

6.6 Off-track skiing

6.7 Fefor and Scott

6.8 Karen Darke

6.9 In Memoriam Waymark Holidays

6.10 Navigation — lost in thought

6.11 Long way home from the snow

6.12 Online applications for XC skiers

SECTION 7: FITNESS TRAINING

7.1 Fitness tests

7.2 The Training Year: Base Training — Endurance

7.3 The Training Year: Base Training — Strength

7.4 The Training Year: Base Training — Speed

7.5 Training for older skiers

7.6 Light on your skis

7.7 A cross-country skier's guide to choosing a gym

7.8 Prehab for skiers

SECTION 8: FITNESS EQUIPMENT

8.1 Nordic Track machines 1

8.2 Wobble boards

8.3 Nordic Track machines 2

8.4 Rollerski maintenance

SECTION 9: NORDIC WALKING

9.1 Not just a stroll in the park

9.2 Hill work with poles

9.3 Nordic walking (advanced)

9.4 Making your own poles

9.5 Nordic walking and biomechanics

SECTION 10: BOOKSHELF

10.1 The Complete Guide to Marathon Walking (D. McGovern)

10.2 Long Distance, a Year of Living Strenuously (B. McKibben)

10.3 Momentum: Chasing the Olympic Dream (P. Vordenberg)

10.4 The First Crossing of Greenland (F. Nansen)

10.5 Worldloppet thirtieth anniversary

10.6 A Medal of Honor (J. Morton)

10.7 Endless Winter — an Olympian's Journal (L. Bodensteiner)

10.8 Books about cross-country skiing — a list for World Book Day

10.9 The Cross-Country Ski, Cook, Look & Pleasure Book (H. Painter)

ABOUT THE AUTHOR

Introduction

Back in 2006 I started to write a blog about cross-country skiing.

In the previous year I had helped to set up a ski travel firm called *XCuk Limited,* and to begin with the articles were intended as a kind of annexe to the Frequently Asked Questions section of the company website. They talked about basic techniques, training, kit & clothing and so on, with a view to helping our customers to prepare for their holiday.

Then things just kind of grew.

By 2013 a total of 180 articles had been posted. Some were ephemeral — news features relating to events that had come and gone. But others seemed to me to be worthy of a wider audience. So I collected together almost 60 of them, edited them to take out occasional repetitiveness and frequent untidy writing, and published them in e-book format. That collection has been well-received and I have been encouraged to produce a paperback edition.

I am interested in lots of aspects of cross-country skiing, and in the blog I always tried to cover a wide range of topics. But I never said much about ski technique. Partly that's because I've never been a very technical skier. But it's also because in 2006 I co-wrote a book called *Stride and Glide: a manual of cross-country skiing and Nordic walking* and I always wanted to avoid repeating topics that had been covered there (by my co-author).

My own history in cross-country skiing started in Scotland in the 1980s, when I took it up as an extension of winter mountaineering. Then, from 1987 until 2005 I was involved with the tour operator Waymark Holidays, initially as a full-time leader and then as part of the management team. In those years I was lucky enough to get lots of skiing — on and off-track — in the Alps, the Pyrenees and Scandinavia.

From 2005 to 2014 our "new" company, *XCuk*, organised holidays and courses in the Alps and Norway. Most winters I was able to ski for four or five weeks.

Section 1
Country Life

Smuksjøseter Fjellstue after a storm

1.1 Fire at Rondvassbu Hut

Posted on 3 February 2008

I'm just back from a week in Høvringen, Norway, with one of our groups. We enjoyed good snow, generally fair weather, and morning temperatures that ranged from plus three to minus eleven. On five out of six days we skied on blue-extra wax. (The other day — the plus three day — was multi-coloured...)

The main news from the area is that the DNT's self-service hut at Rondvassbu has burned down. (The staffed hut is okay.) The fire happened just a day or so before we arrived on Saturday 26 January, and it set in train a remarkable chain of events that affected many people in the area.

The fire was discovered by a small party of British military personnel on a ski-touring exercise. Their route on that day took them from Dørålseter hut, on the north side of the Rondane massif, right into the heart of the mountain range. Their intention was to spend the night in the self-service hut at Rondvassbu, but as they drew near to it they noticed smoke issuing from the hut and by the time they reached the building it was in flames.

One of the soldiers skied down to the nearest settlement (Mysuseter, about 12km away) to raise the alarm. The fire brigade dispatched a crew in a special machine and they quickly extinguished the blaze, but not before it had caused quite serious damage.

As well as the fire brigade, the emergency coordinators also mobilised Roar Skaugen and some of his colleagues. Roar owns the well-known mountain hotel, Smuksjøseter Fjellstue, which lies in a remote spot between Høvringen and Rondvassbu, and he was asked to drive across in one of his caterpillar-tracked vehicles to offer assistance. By the time he started out it was dark and a blizzard had set in.

Unfortunately he strayed a little from the usual track and ditched the vehicle, up-ending it into a deep pool of icy water that flooded into both engine and cabin. The rescue party itself then had to be rescued.

Next day the two machines that prepare the ski tracks in the area were called out to recover Roar's vehicle. One came up from Mysuseter and the other from Høvringen. Together they managed to get Roar's machine out of the watery ditch, but in the process the Høvringen machine sheared the large pin that couples the track-grooming apparatus to the rest of the vehicle. The vehicle could still move around, but it would not be able to groom the tracks until a replacement pin had been found.

One was indeed found, but only after about three days of nationwide searching by the increasingly anxious — and obviously embarrassed — local authorities, who were naturally keen to see the skiing season off to a proper start. The new pin was finally slotted into place at 4 a.m. on the morning of Tuesday 29 January. By the time we were having breakfast on that day the machine was preparing the forest tracks just to the north of our accommodation. Our hotelier, who had started to lay tracks for us with his snow-scooter, could relax.

The cause of the fire is not yet known. Local people told us that another party of skiers had stayed in the hut on the night before the British soldiers discovered the fire, and it was generally supposed that one of them had dropped a cigarette-end into the dry toilet, without realising just how combustible were the materials on to which it would fall. *(In fact they had emptied the wood-stove ashes into the toilet.)*

We skied past Smuksjøseter a few times during the week. Roar made a quick recovery from his icy drenching. And his machine, too, proved quite robust. On our last visit he told me that he expected it back from the workshop the next day, and that the emergency coordinators had agreed to pay for its repair.

The self-service hut at Rondvassbu fared less well. It suffered considerable damage from fire, smoke and water. It will probably need to be demolished and a new one built.

(Footnote: A new hut was indeed opened in October 2008.)

View from Glittertind

1.2 Galdhøpiggen ski race

Posted on 19 April 2009

Last Saturday, 18 April, saw the running of one of the most challenging citizens' ski races in the Norwegian calendar: *Galdhøpiggrennet*. Using Telemark equipment, competitors started near the summit of Galdhøpiggen, now officially Norway's highest mountain (top right in the photo) and descended 1100 metres in altitude over a course that was just 3.5 kilometres in length.

The course was marked with sticks but was not prepared by any kind of grooming machine.

The event takes place each year on the first Saturday after Easter and is based at the lodge at Spiterstulen, in the middle of the Jotunheim mountains. The lodge provides accommodation in bunkrooms and dormitories and it also has a campsite. Usually there about 350 participants though in some years there have been over 400.

Galdhøpiggrennet is a point-and-shoot sort of event, and the winners take only about three minutes. However those in less of a hurry can take up to 45 minutes.

On the way down they pass through stages called Dybvads Horror, Sizziz Schucht, Blue-Ice, and Knee-Shivers. The first section goes over a glacier.

In the Jotunheim you are in a national park and there is no uplift — you need to go up to the start-line on foot, carrying your skis. "Three hours up for three minutes down", says the race organiser's website.

Most of that website is in Norwegian but you can link to a brief summary in English from the home page at *www.galdhopiggrennet.com*.

On the Norwegian pages you can read that the event dates back to 1934, when just 12 skiers took part and the winner recorded a time of 3 minutes and 37 seconds. That time was steadily improved upon until 1948 when Stein Eriksen recorded 2 minutes and 46 seconds. Eriksen went on to win gold in the giant slalom at the 1952 Olympic Games in Oslo, as well as silver in the slalom.

His *Galdhøpiggrennet* record was to stand for 20 years. Then, in the 2007 race two skiers — Eirik Rykhus and Eirik Borgersen shared first place in a time of 2 minutes and 38 seconds

This year's race was again won by Eirik Rykhus — in 2 minutes and 39 seconds, just a second behind his own record. Sunny, cold conditions brought fast times for many other participants, too. Four men finished in under 3 minutes. And the fastest woman wasn't far behind, finishing in 4 minutes and 1 second

Footnote: Until fairly recently there was some dispute over the title to "Norway's Highest Mountain". Galdhøpiggen, which measures 2469m, faced a challenge from nearby Glittertind, which is topped by a glacier and which — depending on prevailing conditions — was sometimes recorded as being higher than Galdhøpiggen. However in recent years Glittertind's glacier has shrunk and the peak is now officially measured at 2465m.

1. 3 Look up! Things to see in the sky

Posted on 18 December 2011

One of *XCuk's* instructors, Kevin H., has a PhD in physics and he usually gives his groups a talk on "Things to see in the sky while out skiing". I've heard it twice and it is fascinating. Recently I've been reading up on the subjects he covers and I've found an excellent website and an interesting, if quirky, book.

The website, titled Atmospheric Optics, is at *www.atoptics.co.uk*. On the homepage it says:

"Light playing on water-drops, dust or ice crystals in the atmosphere, produces a host of visual spectacles — rainbows, halos, glories, coronas and many more. Some can be seen almost every day or so, some are once in a lifetime sights."

The website contains some wonderful photographs, together with brief and lucid descriptions of the various phenomena.

The book is called *The Nature of Light and Colour in the Open Air*. Written by Professor M. Minnaert of the University of Utrecht it was originally published in 1954. I got a paperback edition from Amazon and the blurb tells me that it is an "unabridged reprint of the revised edition of the first translation".

It covers a huge range of phenomena and will leave you with a fond view of the somewhat eccentric professor. You will learn, for example, about the optical payback to be gained from lying underwater on a river bed while a friend "holds a slanting mirror beneath the surface, standing upright in the water and taking special care not to cause ripples". But you will also get a lot of information of a more pertinent and less risky nature.

Anyway, to come back to Kevin's talk, he usually covers the following topics.

Sun dogs

You have most chance of seeing sun dogs when the sun is low in the sky, so a winter's afternoon is a good time. Caused by an ice-halo, which is the result of light bending as it passes through ice crystals in the atmosphere, they appear as bright points of light situated at either side of the sun and in horizontal line with it. (Even with strong sunglasses you'll need to hold up your hands to shield your eyes from the sun itself.)

There is a good image at *www.atoptics.co.uk/halo/parhelia.htm*.

Earth's shadow

Late on a clear day, just after the sun has gone down, the sky to the east will be a beautiful arrangement of colour, shading from dark purple on the horizon to a soft pink higher in the sky. What you are looking at is the shadow of the Earth falling on its own atmosphere.

For a good image, go to *www.atoptics.co.uk/atoptics/earshad.htm*.

Brocken spectre

This is something you can see when you are on a ridge or a hilltop and there is cloud below you. The spectre is your own shadow cast on the cloud, and the outline of the shadow is edged with a "rainbow" effect. In many years of diligent Munro-bagging in Scotland I saw it only twice. When skiing in Europe or Scandinavia you will be very lucky to see it at all, but you have a good chance of glimpsing a similar sort of phenomenon during your flight to the resort, with the aircraft's rainbow-edged shadow cast on cloud below you.

For a good image, go to *www.atoptics.co.uk/droplets/globrock.htm*.

Rainbows

Rainbows are the result of light passing through drops of water, not ice, and on a skiing holiday you are likely to see them only on a sleety day, or when a fine drizzle is falling. (Which is to say, unfortunately, that if you do your skiing in the UK you have a really good chance of seeing them.)

In his book, Minnaert devotes a whole chapter to rainbows and writes about how they are formed, why you sometimes get double rainbows, why the sky *between* two bows is darker than normal and why the sky *inside* the first bow is brighter than normal.

Again, Atmospheric Optics is good: *http://www.atoptics.co.uk/bows.htm*.

The sight of any one of these phenomena can be the psychological high point of a ski holiday, the memory that stays with you, so it's worth taking the time to stop every now and again and just look up. And if you are one of those skiers who persists in staring fixedly at your ski tips as you go along, a bit of sky-gazing might just help you break the habit.

1. 4 Lillehammer Youth Hostel

Posted on 2 September 2012

I tooled the limo into the parking lot, waited five minutes to check I hadn't been followed, and then walked quickly along the subway. In the rail station I rode the elevator to the hostel's second floor. My room seemed as I had left it, the bags apparently undisturbed, but I kept the light off and crossed to the window, stood behind the curtain. Below me the forecourt seemed calm, the early-evening buses coming and going in a normal sort of way, no sign of anyone watching. Everything seemed as it should be. But I was on edge. This was Lillehammer after all, one of the most dangerous cities in the world.

Fanciful? Not if we are to believe the eight-part series of films about to be screened by BBC Four.

Called *Lilyhammer,* the films tell the story of Frank "The Fixer" Tagliano, a New York City mobster who, after testifying in a trial, flees to Lillehammer under the US witness protection program. Once established in his improbable new gaff, Frank (played by Steve Van Zandt of Sopranos and E Street Band fame) introduces the sleepy town to his bad-boy ways. When the series was shown on Norwegian TV last winter, each episode got a million viewers, about a fifth of the population. Hoping for similar success in the UK, BBC Four begins screening it on September 11.

Anyway, to get back to Lillehammer Youth Hostel ... I stayed there for three nights in March while taking a look at some new *XCuk* centres, and my experience might be of interest to anyone searching for budget accommodation close to Norwegian ski areas.

I need to say that I didn't ski while staying at the hostel. Instead I used it as a base from which to drive in a hire car to Venabu, Synnseter and Kamben. Since I had skied at all three places previously I only needed to talk to the owners and see round the properties again, so I left my kit at the hostel (in my room, though I could have used a store-room in the basement).

I also need to say that "budget accommodation" is a relative sort of concept. For three nights B&B in a single room I paid NOK 2085, about GBP 230 at the going rate of exchange. In some countries you could spend your retirement in a hostel for that kind of money.

Lillehammer's hostel is indeed located in the railway station. The reception and café/dining room are on the ground floor of the main station building. Some travellers come in for a coffee before their journey. The bedrooms are on the upper floors of the same building and are reached by a lift and stairs from the ground and basement levels.

My "single" room was a decent-size twin, with shower and toilet. For furniture there was a table and chair and a television (terrestrial only). The outside wall was made almost entirely from glass and overlooked the bus station. I've seldom had such a thoroughly urban view and if I go back I'll ask to be on the other side of the building, overlooking the railway lines but perhaps with a glimpse of distant snowy hills.

Breakfast, the usual sort of Norwegian buffet, was good. And it started at 06.30 which really suited me as I had a lot of driving to do. It would suit skiers, too, as it would allow them an early start.

In the evenings I could have bought dinner in the hostel café, or used the members' kitchen. But I preferred to call into a shopping centre on the edge of town and buy the bread-and-cheese-and-beer sort of provisions. I could then write up my notes while eating. If I had been skiing I would probably have tried to eat up at the ski grounds, in Verthuset café at Sjusjøen for example, and then come down to Lillehammer on a late bus.

The great thing about the hostel is that it is handily located. After breakfast you can walk out the door and take your choice of buses to several very good places for skiing. The times in brackets are departure times from Lillehammer: Sjusjøen (09.00), Nordseter (07.50 and 09.00), Skeikampen (08.45 and 09.20), Hafjell (09.20).

No matter how handy its location, you are unlikely to want to spend a lot of time at the hostel. A week would be much too long. But if you had a couple of days before or after another holiday and planned to do some exploring it would be a good bet. Equally, if you were shopping for ski kit it would make a convenient base.

Some skiers stay there on the nights before and after races. I arrived the day after the Birkebeiner marathon and several racers were checking out just as I was checking in. It would also be good for the Troll Ski Marathon.

If you are at all a nervous traveller you need to be warned that there is no security — none — between the station and the rooms. Anyone can gain access to the corridor outside your room. I seemed to be the only person who was concerned about this. Each morning there were other lone travellers in the breakfast-bar, women as well as men, and everyone appeared relaxed. When I spoke to the hostel manager about it, he said there was never a problem: although some drunks now and again come into the station, the police operate zero-tolerance and immediately cart them off.

And that is reassuring. But nastier beings than drunks do exist and even safe countries like Norway have their share of them. So an extra security door or two might be worth the investment. And now that the town is to be the resort of Mafia hoodlums, it might just be wise to make them bullet-proof.

1.5 Mountain transport in Høvringen

Posted on 24 April 2013

This winter I was lucky enough to get four weeks' skiing in Norway. One of them was at Høvringen, on the edge of Rondane National Park. As usual we began one of the day-tours with a ride in our hotel's ancient snowcat (a Bombardier half-track with caterpillar and skis). And as usual it was a popular outing.

Most of us opted for one of the 12 places listed on the sign-up sheet as *In*, but two hardier souls chose to go *Ut*, which meant they kept their skis on and were towed behind.

We liked the spectacle and the quirkiness every bit as much as the actual journey. So our cameras flashed and videos rolled while the machine trundled into the hotel car park. They continued to flash and roll while we loaded skis and poles on to the roof-rack and loaded ourselves into the cabin. And they were busy again when we climbed out at about 1150m on a spectacular plateau 5km from the hotel. My own camera was as busy as anybody else's, and I put some images and a video on *XCuk's* Facebook page. (Later I put an extended video on YouTube.)

The machine belongs to Arne Hovengen who runs our hotel (Øigardseter Fjellstue) and I asked him to tell me about it. It was a bit like asking a man about his newly-born son: he answered my questions with obvious pride.

Arne sometimes calls the machine the *beltebil* and sometimes the *weasel*. But properly speaking it is a Bombardier Snowmobile (he doesn't know if it has a specific model name). It was made in Quebec in 1956 and has a 6.2 litre V8 diesel engine. When he first bought it, it had a 6-cylinder Chrysler petrol engine. But he changed it because of difficulty in getting spares. ("A man down in the valley rebuilt it for me.")

He bought it from a bus company that had used it for transporting people in the Femund area, near Røros. (Rural depopulation gradually made the service uneconomic and finally it stopped operating.)

It is Arne's fourth machine. His first one, many years ago, was a Muskeg. It was mainly designed for industrial use — carrying material rather than people — and although it was very strong it was rather too slow. Then he got a Bombardier with wooden carriage-work but it proved too narrow and tippy for the rough tracks around Høvringen. He stopped using it but kept it for spares. Next he bought a Snowcat with a VW engine, but it was too small.

He feels that the present Bombardier is just right and he has no plans to change it. "It will last as long as I do". He keeps it going through regular servicing. Now and again something needs to be replaced. As the nearest source of spare parts is a factory in Canada, he keeps a good supply in his workshop, especially roller wheels and cat tracks. Sometimes he has bodged a replacement from car parts. In extremis he calls upon his friend, the man down in the valley. ("If he can't fix it, he knows a good blacksmith who can.")

Vehicles like Arne's are becoming an endangered species in Norway. He estimates that there are now only 25 working machines in the entire country. In total, six of them are in or near Høvringen. (Smuksjøseter Fjellstue has two. Putten Seter has one. Høvringen Høyfjellshotell has two.)

The decline is partly due to cost: they are expensive. Bombardier no longer makes people-carriers and a decent second-hand one will set you back half a million kroner. You could have a brand new 4WD car, a hefty one, for half as much. Just as importantly, the use of such machines is heavily restricted in Norway. You need a permit, and they seem to be harder and harder to obtain.

Arne had problems with his own permit-renewal last year. By the time the new licence actually made it through his letterbox, very little of its nominal 12-month period was left to run. Roar Haugen, owner of nearby Smuksjøseter Fjellstue, had the same problem even though his business absolutely depends on his snowcats. Pooling their resources the pair therefore mounted a campaign that took them first to the Environment Ministry and then to the Parliament itself. It was a tough fight, but they now have lifetime permits.

Section 2
Skiing with Children

2.1 Barnas Holmenkolldag

Posted on 2 March 2008

Today the 35th annual *Barnas Holmenkolldag* takes place in Norway. A huge cross-country ski festival for children, it is based up at Holmenkollen, a very popular ski area just to the north of Oslo city. The event usually attracts around 8,000 young participants.

The day is intended for children aged between four and twelve years and aims to encourage youngsters to take part in cross-country skiing through a mix of low-key races and fun events.

Although the event is often billed as the world's biggest ski race for children, the "races" are hardly recognisable as such. They are deliberately non-competitive. Performances are not timed. Instead, the tracks are kept open for a period of several hours, during which the children go round them when they like and at their own pace.

There are four tracks, aimed at different age-groups. The youngest children (four to five years) can tackle a 250m circuit within the main stadium. Those aged from five to seven can do a 1000m circuit. Seven to twelve year-olds can choose between the 3km Short Elk Loipe and the 5km Long Elk Loipe.

All the tracks are prepared for classic style.

When the children have had enough skiing, they can take part in lots of other activities. There is a temporary farm with horses, calves and goats. There are dramatic stage productions. There are stalls selling (and sometimes giving away) food and clothing. There are Lapp tepees to shelter in. There is ski fun in a "ski park". Children also have free entrance to the ski museum.

Barnas Holmenkolldag encapsulates some really good principles for skiing with young children. A fundamental one is that even *very* young children can find cross-country skiing enjoyable — but only if it is pitched at the correct level.

Key to achieving the correct level is keeping things short. In the main, children don't have a grown-up aesthetic for the majestic wilderness, so while adults might enjoy a long, silent foray through snowy forest and o'er mighty peak, young kids will generally find it tedious in the extreme. They want their time on skis to be episodic.

And they want things to be fun. A major part of what they are experiencing is simply the discovery of snow, a magical substance with limitless scope for play. They will want to have snowball fights, to build snowmen, tunnels, caves and castles — and simply to roll about in the drift. And they will, eventually, want to go out on skis, but even then they will prefer to ski in a playful way rather than simply covering distance for the sake of going far.

At Holmenkollen some formal skiing instruction will be available. But there will be a much stronger emphasis on allowing children to improve their own skills in specially designed "ski parks". These are areas in which prepared tracks lead over a variety of natural challenges provided by the terrain itself: climbs, descents, twists and turns. To these are added man-made challenges like bumps and jumps, slalom poles and gates. Simply by getting round the course, the children will be developing their ski technique.

Barnas Holmenkolldag is organised by Skiforeningen — the Association for the Promotion of Skiing. One of Skiforeningen's other responsibilities is to organise the *adult* racing season at Holmenkollen, which includes world-class events attracting elite competitors. So they may secretly hope that some of the youngsters enjoying today's activities will one day stand on a winner's podium.

But they know that they have to go slowly.

All sports show high rates of drop-out among children, and one of the times of greatest risk is soon after a child has been identified as a promising future prospect. The activity that was once a carefree pleasure can easily turn into a chore. The answer is to try to keep the focus on fun until, ideally, the mid-teenage years. Only then should dedicated training start.

2.2 Skiing with children — a cautionary tale

Posted on 27 February 2013

I've just spent a week cross-country skiing with my son, now 12 years old. It was a nice holiday, and a big contrast to the first time I ever skied with children, in the early 1990s, when I worked for Waymark Holidays. The account of that first time was written up for another publication and is reproduced below. It's a little rude — you are warned.

Christmas at Kvitåvatn

"Hey, Rod! Mary Ellen says you've got a twelve-inch willy!"

I heard about it a couple of hours afterwards and decided that the time to be disappointed rather than angry had well and truly passed.

"Why did you say that, you little bastard?"

There were tears in his eyes. He was having difficulty getting the words out.

I loosened my grip on his throat.

"Because Mary Ellen did say it, and my Dad says I should always tell the truth."

"Tell the truth one more time and you're dead! Got that?"

The hearer of my words was an angel-faced boy of eight. We'll call him John. He was a member of my extended family and his parents had been finding his recent behaviour rather challenging.

Perhaps still influenced by my social work days, I had felt that his school had over-reacted when they suspended him. Okay, it had been wrong for John and his classmates to lob their lunchtime pizza crusts into the pram in the nearby garden, but how were they to know there was a baby in it?

I knew from my own admittedly distant experience that school discipline could sometimes be wrongheaded. At about John's age I'd been carpeted for attempting a judo throw on an elderly female teacher. I had argued that I was just trying to free myself from her grip, a jujitsu choke now favoured by Brazilian cage-fighters. My brother, too, had had an unequal brush with authority. Deciding at an early stage that he didn't like this new school (we had just moved from another town) he escaped from the classroom and fled for home, a misdemeanour that led the Headmistress to wrap him in brown paper and string. (I wish I was making this up. Recently I asked him if he remembered the incident. "Remember it? I still get the nightmares.")

So I was willing to give John the benefit of the doubt. He was simply a little confused. A nice holiday in the countryside, with lots of fresh air, will sort him out, I said to his mum, naively sharing the error of many well-intenders before and since.

Accordingly, we were now on a ten-night holiday at Kvitåvatn Fjellstoge, in Norway's Telemark region, and I was the ski-school teacher for the middle group, aged six to ten. John was my guest. Mary Ellen was another eight-year-old member of our group. It was a new venture for Waymark, our first "family holiday", and I was immensely keen for it to succeed.

Kvitåvatn had been established in the nineteen-seventies by Rod Tuck, formerly a captain in the Royal Marines, formerly an Olympic biathlete, and forever a man of considerable dignity and bearing. Many of the buildings had gone up through his own hard labour and he was justifiably proud of the place. So he liked to show guests around, in a tall vice-regal sort of way.

With a deep cultured voice he would recount how in the first days there was nothing up here but savage wilderness, how he and a couple of associates had cleared the barren ground, laid the foundations, raised the walls, put on the roofs. Then he would move along to the cluster of old *seter* buildings he had saved from destruction and had brought here — log by log — in his ancient trusty bus, determined to salvage for Posterity these relics of the bygone upland way of life.

All this would take rather a long time and when next he went on to tell of how he had excavated the duck-pond and built the tractor-shed, even the most resolute of his adult listeners might be shuffling their feet. Eight year-old boys would certainly be growing restless.

"Hey Rod! Mary Ellen says ..."

Rod never really spoke to me after that, perhaps rightly concluding that I should not have let the boy out of my sight. But it was now the mid-point of the holiday and one of the other instructors had kindly offered to look after the kids for a couple of hours, to allow me ski off some pent-up steam. It was just unfortunate that Rod had chosen that precise time to offer his guided tour.

And it wasn't only Rod that now kept out of my way. Some of the clients also avoided me and when one evening John and I sat down at a dinner table the man already occupying it got up abruptly and, clutching his plate, strode determinedly off to the most distant corner of the dining room.

On my one previous visit to Kvitåvatn, some years earlier, there had been a parrot loose in the building, the ostentatious pet of one of a gang of ostentatious NATO staffers, up from Oslo. They had arrived by car just before my own group came down from the mountains in the dying light.

It had been bitterly cold even before we skied through the super-chilled mist gathering over the lake, and when we came into the lodge we looked impressively rugged, with ice in our hair, eyebrows and beards. One man — Number Eleven, we called him — had long frozen tusks on account of his daylong refusal to wipe his nose. So our meeting with the parrot seemed a little outlandish. Maybe it was a cockatoo. I can't remember and it doesn't matter. What matters is that for several days the damn thing shot about the place from beam to rafter, dropping feathers and noxious substances, obliging everyone to shelter their coffee cups, to duck their heads, and in general to be warily and continuously on guard. It had seemed remarkable that so small a creature could cause such great upheaval.

Which brings me back to John. The Rod episode was the culmination of several days of trauma. My list of Things-Not-To-Do had somehow changed into a list of challenges. The sauna had been on it, yet when one evening John went AWOL that's where I eventually found him, on the top bench and as red as a lobster. The upper reaches of the nursery piste were also *verboten* — "just till you've learned the proper techniques" — yet that's where he was inexorably drawn, and would come screeching down at terminal velocity, narrowly escaping multiple collisions, scattering people in all directions and one time thumping into the side of a hut. Fighting with the other kids had not initially been on the list, but was added when a clash of personalities was resolved using Kung Fu.

It was all a far cry from the picture I'd started out with: skiing with rosy-faced youngsters over glistening snowfields, filling their eager minds with a love and respect for Nature, watching them eat hearty, nutritious meals then go contentedly off to early beds.

Mind you, it wasn't a rose garden for the other leaders either. We'd omitted to provide Lego for the under-fives. Okay, we had provided a qualified carer and a cosy room and we had provided a lot of indoor and outdoor toys. But we hadn't provided Lego. And that was *catastrophic* for one of the children, who simply couldn't get through her day without the little coloured bricks. At each lunch break her distraught mother would have to console her, several times greatly delaying her own ski-group's restart.

In the top group some of the adults complained about skiing with the teenagers, because they forced the pace, made a racket and threw snowballs. And the teenagers retaliated by saying that the adults were too slow, too boring and too grumpy.

And, undeniably, Mary Ellen could be a bit of a handful.

We decided not to offer any more family holidays. There were easier ways to make a living.

Several months later — my blood-pressure had just about stabilised — I got a call from John's mother. He and his chums had been playing Chicken, in an unwise contest between children on bicycles and adults in cars, and he had fetched up in hospital with a broken jaw. As it turned out, it was the best thing that could have happened. Brought up face-to-face, as it were, with his own destructibility he calmed down, settled in at his studies, even had a poem published in the school magazine. Today, a grown man, he's a veritable pillar of the community.

But we're still not close.

Section 3
Skiing Tips for Beginners

3.1 Half snowplough

Posted on 18 May 2006

You use the half snowplough for slowing down or stopping when skiing in tracks. It's a really important technique, because until you are confident you can stop, you won't be at all keen to let your skis glide, even on flat ground. And you will certainly be wary of starting down even the gentlest of slopes.

When skiing in tracks you should always ski in the right-hand track, and you use your left ski to brake. The left ski is lifted out of the track, then stemmed into a wedge shape and placed on the central part of the track. It sounds easy, but it is actually very challenging for newcomers, as it combines several movements and — scariest of all — involves moving all of your weight on to one ski.

When learning the technique it is useful to break it down into six different elements, and to work on them one-by-one. It is vital to select the right terrain for this. You need a stretch of track that slopes downward enough to allow you to ski down it without poling. The slope also needs to "run out" on to flat ground, so that you will come to a safe stop even if you do nothing to slow yourself down. Ideally the slope should be preceded by a flat stretch of track, on which you can get into the correct position before setting off downhill, and in the following descriptions I have assumed that you have indeed been able to find such a slope.

Element 1: Straight running down a gently-sloping track
Adopt a position in which:

- your feet are in the track grooves, and are thus about hip-width apart
- your knees are slightly bent (your knees should be above and in line with your big toes)
- your upper body is inclined slightly forward from the hips
- your shoulders are relaxed and your hands are held slightly in front of you and slightly out to the sides of your body

We will call this your "basic position". Maintaining this basic position, allow yourself simply to slide down the slope on your skis. Repeat this several times, feeling your confidence grow each time.

Element 2: Shift weight on to right foot
Soon you are going to lift your left ski clear of the snow. In order to be able to do that, you have to take your body weight off of it, and transfer almost all your weight on to your right ski.

So, starting from your basic position, shift most of your weight on to your right foot. In doing this you will move your right hip to the right, so that your right foot, right knee and right hip are in line vertically. Ensure that your weight is over the whole of your right foot (not back on to the heel or forward on to the ball of the foot).

Maintaining this new right-weighted position, allow yourself to run down the slope. Repeat this several times, feeling your confidence grow each time.

Element 3: Lift left ski clear of the snow
When you are happy with the right-weighted position, lift your left ski out of its groove, taking it no more than a couple of inches off the snow.

Keep it pointing forward, in the same direction as the track. (Don't try to wedge it yet.) After a couple of seconds, place it back into the groove.

Practise this as you go down the slope, lifting and lowering the left ski. Keep your weight on your right ski all the time. Repeat this several times. As your confidence grows, try to lift your left ski up for longer periods each time. If you get really confident you can try to ski all the way down your slope on just your right ski.

Element 4: *Place left ski on to the snow in a wedge*

Maintaining the right-weighted position, lift your left ski as just described in Element 3. Now lay it on the snow in a wedge shape, pushing your left heel out to the side. Do not put any body weight on to it.

Your right ski still points forward in its track. And your left ski tip comes close to the right ski tip.

At this stage don't worry about how wide the wedge is. As long as your ski tails are further apart than your ski tips, you are making progress.

Now lift your left ski up again and place it back into its track.

Go down the slope several times practising the sequence: lift; wedge; replace in track.

Element 5: *Move your weight gradually over on to the left ski*

This time, when you have wedged your left ski, move some of your body weight on to it. Do this gently and progressively. Concentrate on moving from the hip, keeping your upper body relaxed.

Feel your weight pressing down through the centre of your left foot.

You will feel all your upper body moving from its right-weighted position, through a more central position, and gradually to a left-weighted position.

Go down your slope several times practising this. You will feel the wedge getting a little wider as your weight shifts to the left.

Element 6: *Bring the left ski gradually on to its inside edge*

This last element calls for a gentle touch, and before trying it you should feel happy with Elements 1 to 5.

This time, when you have wedged and weighted your left ski, push the *inside* edge of the left ski down and into the snow. You do this by lowering your left knee a little, and then pushing downwards and outwards with the inside edge of your left foot. You should come to a stop!

The above sequence will be very challenging for most beginners, and they will not be able to manage it in a single session. Instead, they should come back to their slope on several successive days, for maybe an hour per day, and each time just do as much as they can. If on the first day they can get only as far as Element 3, say, then that is fine — maybe they'll be able to manage Element 4 on the next day. They can still go out and enjoy some skiing, but until they can manage the entire sequence they should stay on flat ground.

3.2 Going faster (by not going so slowly)

Posted on 22 May 2006

Newcomers to XC skiing typically want to concentrate on learning how to go slowly, how to stay in control. But there comes a point when you want to go faster. Okay, maybe you don't want to enter races, but you would prefer to be towards the front of your group rather than the back, and you would also like to feel a little less tired at the end of the day.

Improvements in technique are obviously important here. But a good supplementary strategy is to identify all the things that are making you go slowly and then change or eliminate them.

Make sure you are not "choking" your diagonal stride

Your skis are designed to glide. They want to glide. So let them glide. Many skiers adopt an arm-leg tempo that is too quick, and in doing so they interrupt the natural glide of the skis. Experiment with this.

Find a stretch of flat track and mark off a length of about 50 metres — use trees or poles as markers or simply leave a rucksack at either end. Now ski along the length of track and count double strides (count your left or your right foot each time). Let's imagine you take 30 double strides to complete the stretch. Your goal now is to reduce that by 10 per cent. So, ski along the same length of track until you can do it in 27 double strides. You will need to lengthen your stride — and let your skis glide. Maybe you'll need to pole a little harder, too. Next, when you can consistently manage the stretch in 27 strides, aim to reduce it further to 25 strides.

Let your skis glide down the hills
As your confidence improves you will naturally apply the brakes less strongly and less often. You will not need to be told that this will result in an increase in speed! But you might not realise just how important the downhill speed is in taking you up and over any small bumps that you encounter in the middle of your descent or at the bottom of it — bumps that would otherwise cost you energy and time. You will also not need to be told that snowploughing is hard work and that the less of it you can do, the less tired will be your leg muscles at the end of the day. Confidence is the vital factor. So, if you want to go faster — learn how to slow down. Work on your half snowplough until it is bomb-proof. When you are certain you can rely on it, you will be less inclined to apply it.

If you have your own skis, take a look at the bases
The tips and tails (the front and back thirds of your skis) are the areas on which you glide. And you will glide better if they are properly base-waxed. Unfortunately many XC skiers neglect this. If you don't want to base-wax them yourself, get a shop to do it for you. And if that isn't possible then a quick and dirty solution is to crayon thin layers of "Polar" grip wax on to the tips and tails and cork it in, taking care to use a clean cork.

Make sure you ski with your skis flat to the snow
People who run or jog are used to the likelihood that when they plant their foot it will not be flat to the ground. Some people naturally turn their foot out slightly and come on to its outside edge. Others turn their foot inwards and come on to the inside edge. Manufacturers of running shoes cater for this variety by designing shoes for "neutral" gait and for those who excessively "pronate" or "supinate".

The same variety of foot-placement can happen when cross-country skiing, and it can make you turn slightly on to the edge of your skis, even when skiing on flat ground. And that will slow you down. Ski-boot manufacturers do not really cater for this, so it is up to you to watch your skiing style and to try to ensure that your ski base is always flat to the snow. (Remember, too, that beginners often ski a little on their edges because of anxiety: an instinct for self-preservation can make you slightly knock-kneed, which brings you on to your inside edges, and slows you down.)

Make sure you are not resting when you could be working

Imagine that you are coming to an uphill section of track. A beginner might approach it slowly, ski halfway up using diagonal stride, and then stop for a rest before continuing to the top in a herringbone or sidestep action. A slightly more advanced skier would get all the way to the top using diagonal stride, and then stop for a rest before continuing. However a seasoned skier would get all the way to the top using diagonal stride and would then keep going, but at a relaxed pace — resting through "active recovery". You can save a lot of time by resting on the move, rather than stopping.

Eradicate rucksack-faffing

An accomplished rucksack-faffer can cost a group an hour a day. I remember leading beginners' holidays in an Austrian resort where sometimes the loipe crossed roads and we would need to remove our skis and walk across. One client would each time arrive sweating at the road, and would then stop and take off her large jacket and slowly squash it into her small rucksack. She would then take off her skis and walk across the road. By the time she got to the other side and had clipped back into her skis, she would have become cold. So she would take off the rucksack again and slowly extricate her jacket and put it back on. At length we would be ready to go, and would start off along the loipe once again, looking forward to the next road-crossing…

As well as dressing appropriately, experienced skiers learn to think ahead. When they come to a rest stop they have a mental list of things to do: take food and drink, put on a little more wax, change hats. You don't need to be obsessive about this — you are on holiday after all — but you want to avoid (for example) repacking your rucksack at the end of a snack stop, clipping back into your skis, and only then deciding to take a photograph (for which you will need your camera, which is hidden somewhere deep in your rucksack).

3. 3 Downhill skills

Posted on 24 February 2009

In Norway recently I was instructing on our Back to Basics course, at Dalseter. We had described it in the brochure like this:

This course is for those who already have at least a week's experience of cross-country skiing but feel that they have not yet quite mastered the basic skills. It is for people who still feel a little wobbly on their skis, and who find a moderately fast descent a scary prospect rather than an exciting one.

Naturally enough the participants wanted to work on their downhill skills. Mainly we focussed on the bread and butter stuff: the snowplough and its variants.

Half snowplough brake

You use this for slowing down or stopping when skiing in grooved tracks. We described a teaching progression for it in the posting of 18 May 2006 (see Chapter 3.1) where we broke the move down into six different elements:

Element 1 Straight run down a gently sloping track.

Element 2 Shift most of body weight on to right foot.

Element 3 Lift left ski clear of the snow.

Element 4 Place left ski on the snow in a wedge.

Element 5 Move body weight gradually over on to the left ski.

Element 6 Bring the left ski gradually on to its inside edge.

Common faults in the Dalseter group were:

• Not having a good basic position: usually standing too stiff and too tall. Ideally the knees should be slightly bent, and they should be above and in line with the big toes. And the upper body should be inclined slightly forward from the hips.

• Keeping shoulders tight and hands high.

• Not shifting body weight sufficiently during elements 2 and 5.

Full snowplough brake

This is for stopping when there is no groove in the track. You slide both skis out into a wedge shape. We used a safe area of the hotel's downhill piste for practice. Common faults in our group were:

• Again, keeping shoulders tight and hands high. This can shift your weight forward on to the balls of your feet, increasing the chance that you will fall on your face.

• Sitting back. This is the opposite of the previous fault. It puts your weight on to your heels, increasing the chance that you will fall on your back.

• Not using any inside edge. This can make you drift out into a wider and wider (and more and more uncomfortable) wedge. The answer is to apply a little inside edge by slightly dropping your knees, in a subtle movement.

• Weighting too much on one side. This makes you veer off toward the edge of the slope, instead of going straight down it. The best way to deal with this, during a practice-session, is just to let it happen. Regard it as a good snowplough turn, rather than as a bad snowplough brake. Once you have practised a few turns to each side you should have learned enough control to be able to go straight down the hill.

Snowplough turns

We used the belly-button torch method. When you want to turn to one side, imagine your belly-button is a torch and that you are going to use it to illuminate your proposed route. You turn your body so as to shine the torch in the direction you want to go. Doing this should keep your weight on the correct ski, and should counteract the tendency to steer with your shoulders.

Again we practised on the piste. We progressed to wider radius turns, breaking the move into a *traverse phase* (in which you stand up, with your skis parallel) and a *turning phase* (in which you sink down, with your skis in a wedge).

Common faults were:

• Trying to steer by rotating the shoulders. (This can put your weight precisely on to the wrong ski.)

• Not allowing the turn to complete sufficiently, and therefore standing up too early into the next traverse. This isn't in itself a bad thing, but it does make you go down the hill in quick, short-radius turns. And when your problem is one of confidence, that's not such a helpful thing to do.

Learning to enjoy the speed

We did this by:

• Moving progressively up the slope on which we were working, to give ourselves a longer run down.

• Standing up for longer in the traverse phase (which also helps you to sink lower in the turn phase).

Our "ski-school" sessions lasted about an hour and a half at a time. Any longer and the students started to lose interest — or to regress — at which stage it was better to go for a tour and try to put the new skills into practice.

Section 4
Equipment and Waxing

4.1 End of season tidy-up

Posted on 21 April 2007

Most years I get home from the last ski trip of the season and straightaway throw all my kit into the garage, promising myself I'll get around to sorting it out "very soon". And there it will lie untouched for months, until the approach of Christmas provokes a panic. But this season — I'm getting old — I had most of it sorted away within a few days of arriving home. Here is a list of the jobs that needed doing.

Skis

I like to base-wax my skis before the summer lay-off. I can do this at home, but I'm not especially well set-up for it and this year I managed to do it during my last trip to Norway. The hotel (in Høvringen) had a heated ski-hut equipped with waxing bench and iron. In my ski bag I found some old racing base-wax, a relic from a past Engadin marathon and therefore a bit incongruous when dripped on to my mountain skis; but the main thing at this time of year is just to get some kind (any kind) of wax into the bases, so I was happy to use it. The hot-wax job took about an hour. Then after a quick check of the bindings the skis were ready to go into the ski-bag — except that the ski-bag was torn.

Ski-bag

One day I'll get around to reinforcing properly the ends of my ski-bags, which are invariably the sections that get damaged. For now I've used duct tape. If it starts to curl up I'll stick it with a seam sealant.

Boots

I've used only my touring boots this season (no time for track skiing). They are made from leather, and before putting them away for the summer I applied a generous layer of leather wax, both inside and out.

Poles

When skiing off-track I use Swix Mountain poles. I saw three such poles fail this season, all breaking at the basket. So I took extra care to rub leather wax on the basket-straps (as well as the hand-straps) before storing them.

Climbing skins

My skins got a lot of use this year. So an application of glue was in order before they went into the cupboard.

Waxes

I cleaned all the grip-wax tubs with solvent, and did my scrapers at the same time. I put all the partly-used klister tubes into sealable plastic bags. I then packed the lot away in my waxing box.

Rucksack

When travelling by air I always tie up my main rucksack in a swathe of rock-climbing tape before entrusting it to the baggage handlers. This certainly impedes their remorseless, unswerving mission to reduce it to tatters — but they still nevertheless manage every time to burst at least one of the plastic strap-buckles. That wouldn't be such a problem if I could find replacements that were compatible with the originals. Then I could just renew the half of the buckle that was broken; and usually the half that gets broken is the "male" half, which you can replace simply by threading a new one on to the loose webbing.

But I always have to fit a complete new buckle — which means replacing the "female" half as well. Doing that properly would be an impossibly fiddly task, as I would have to unpick maybe half a metre of stitching in the webbing, and then sew it all back up afterwards. Life is just too short.

However there is a workaround. What you have to do is take the end of the new female half of the buckle — the end that you would have sewn into the webbing if you could have been bothered to unpick it — and then cut through its plastic bar at about 45 degrees, so that you can slide it on to the webbing. You need a hacksaw and a soft vice. And you need a lot of care, otherwise you'll break the buckle and cut off your finger. It helps if you make the cut a little to one side of the centre of the plastic bar: this makes it easier to slide it on to the loop of webbing.

Spare parts and handy things

While out skiing most of us have all sorts of brainwaves, about things we should have remembered to bring or inventions we could surely patent. (The waxable loipe is just not feasible — forget it.) It is useful to put together a little box of bits and pieces before your memories fade. Into my own box this season will go:

- One or two pre-cut plastic buckles, as described above.
- Some re-usable cable-ties, for running repairs to kit.
- Two spare baskets for my poles. (I bought a pair in the shop in Høvringen.)
- Spare climbing skins.
- A couple of miniature plastic bottles, the kind the airlines give you for your inflight vodka-martini. They are good for holding small quantities of wax-removing solvent, and for shampoo, and are especially useful if you are on a moving-along tour. (It is of course quite a good idea to re-label the bottles accordingly...)

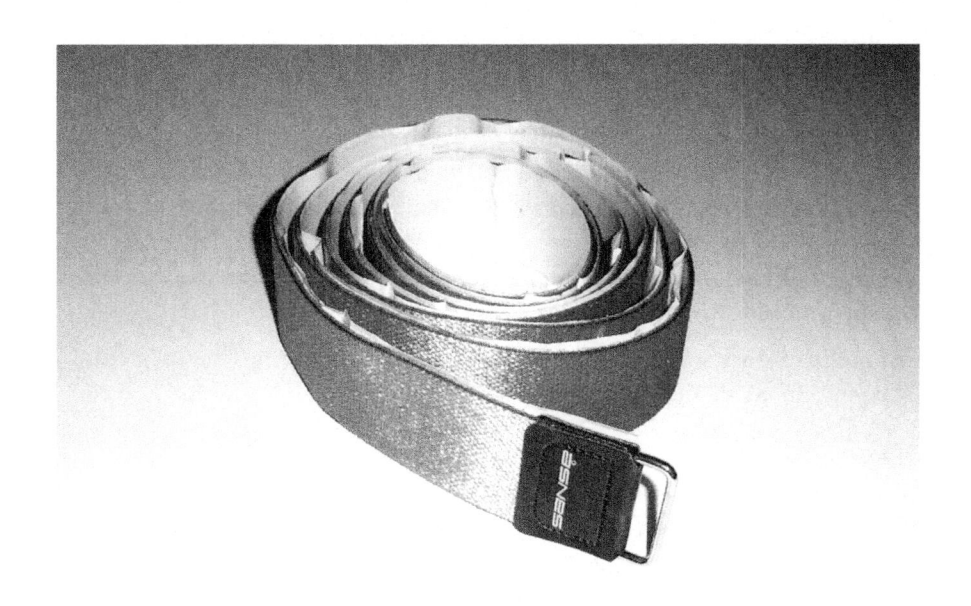

4.2 Choosing climbing skins

Posted on 25 November 2007

In preparation for the winter season, and spurred on by the recent heavy snowfall in Norway, we are presently building up our stock of climbing skins. (We rent them out to clients on some of our off-track holidays.)

This posting outlines the sort of things we have had to consider in deciding what to buy. Maybe it will help those of you who are intending to buy your own skins.

We have changed our thinking about climbing skins over the last couple of seasons. At first we didn't want to use them at all on our holidays. This was because we felt (and still feel) that the growth in use of skins during the 1990s led relatively inexperienced skiers on to terrain that was too difficult for them. The skins allowed them to climb up hills that were longer and steeper than they could confidently ski back down. Recently, however, our own groups have often experienced tricky, glazed conditions in which skins can be more appropriate than waxes, even on fairly gentle ground. In response to this we have decided to build up a stock of general purpose skins that will be suitable for valley touring as well as for bagging the occasional Munro.

Choice of material

Skins used to be made from seal-skin, hence the name, and the principle was that the hairs in the seal's fur would stay flat to the snow if moved in one direction, and would therefore glide, but would rise up, and would therefore grip, if moved in the other direction. Nowadays the choice is between synthetic materials, which are very durable, and mohair, which has good gliding properties. And you can get a mohair/synthetic mix that balances the advantages of both.

For our own stock we have given precedence to durability and have chosen 100 per cent synthetic.

Width

Skins come in several widths. The standard advice that you'll get from most shops and suppliers is to choose skins that are almost as wide as your skis. And that certainly makes sense when you intend to go straight up the sides of mountains that have sustained slopes. So if your chosen terrain is the high Alps, you should opt for wide skins.

However, on more unevenly graded hillsides and on rolling terrain — classic Norwegian conditions — narrower skins are useful. They give sufficient grip for the climbs, but they still allow you some glide when you come to flat or down-sloping sections. So they are not as hard work as wide skins. For our own purposes, the narrower skins are best, and we have therefore opted for a width of 35mm.

Type of fitting

Some skins are designed to attach to the ski at *both* tip and tail. Normally these have a rubberised fitting at either the tip end or the tail end, to help keep the skin tightly in place. The principle is a good one. But the problem is that these rubberised sections can break — as we know from bitter experience. And once they have broken it can be almost impossible to make running repairs to them. So we have gone for the simpler models, which fix only to the ski tip, by means of a metal clip.

4.3 When skis ball-up

Posted on 24 January 2008

It is turning into quite a snowy winter. Since November there have been frequent blizzards in Scandinavia and in many parts of the Alps. Closer to home, Scotland is having one of its best seasons for years.

One of the downsides of skiing in fresh snow — we're never happy — is that the bases of your skis can ball-up. At worst you end up with high stilts of compacted snow under your grip zones, which make any progress impossible. More commonly you get a patch of snow or ice sticking to just one ski, which messes up your rhythm and knocks you off balance.

Here are some tips on how to prevent your skis from balling-up; and on how to cope if it does happen.

Ski care

Firstly, irrespective of whether you are using waxable or waxless skis, you need to keep their bases clean. All skis pick up dirt from the ski-trails. They will also gather road dirt if you carry them on a bus rack, as well as gathering wax and klister from other skis on the rack. All this can make the skis sticky, so you should clean them every day or so, using solvent.

If you are using waxless skis with fish-scale bases, then be ready for the fish-scales to ball-up as soon as it starts to snow (and probably also for a day or two after that). You should buy a tin of fish-scale glide spray from a ski shop and apply it before you set out, and then again as and when you need it. Apply it sparingly. You often see beginners using half a tin in one go, but a thin application is all that's needed.

If you have waxable skis then it is more than usually important to make sure that your grip wax is not too warm for the conditions. On any day the mnemonic for grip waxing is: *Thicker, Longer, Change (TLC)*. On a snowy day it can pay to start with a wax that is slightly too cold for the prevailing temperature. It may in fact work very well. However, if you do get poor grip you should add another layer of the same wax (*Thicker*). If you still get poor grip, you should add a *Longer* layer of the same wax. And only if, after all that, you still have poor grip, should you *Change* to a warmer wax.

Care when skiing

When you are in tracks that have fresh snow on them, you should keep your skis moving and try not to stop too often. Always move your skis by sliding then — avoid lifting them. If you do come to a halt, try to avoid coming out of the track grooves. (This advice contravenes the rules of the track, so only follow it if there are no other skiers around.)

If you do come to a halt, plant your poles to your sides for balance and then lift up one ski at a time and bang it down and forward on to the track, to clear off any adhering snow. Remember the forward part of the movement — it's like an aeroplane (bumpily) landing, not a helicopter.

When snow conditions are sticky it can be useful to ski in the style adopted by many Norwegian tourers. They lead from the knee, each stride involving a pronounced forward down-sink with the knee, as if they were trying to crush something under the ball of their foot. This technique looks a bit weird, but it certainly helps keep your ski bases clean.

The wrong skis?

If one person in a group is consistently having greater problems than the others, it may be because his or her skis are too soft or too short. In that case a hire shop should be able to help by issuing a stiffer or a longer pair. But be careful of putting a *beginner* on to stiffer or longer skis. You may stop the balling-up, but you'll also make the skier travel faster when going down hills, which is seldom what a beginner wants. (Some beginners go around with huge backpacks, whose weight can flatten their skis excessively. Lightening the load can of itself solve the problem.)

Alternatively, as a workaround, use the TLC stratagem in reverse. Ask the struggling skier to apply wax in a manner that is thinner, shorter and colder than everyone else.

If you are using *wooden* skis and they are balling-up, then the answer might lie in careful choice and application of grip-wax, as described above. But there may be another problem — your bases might need to be re-tarred. If you can't get access to the kit required for this, you can sometimes improvise a short-term remedy by rubbing the affected parts of the bases with a very cold grip wax (green or polar) or even with candle-wax. All you are trying to do is seal the bases, and thus prevent untreated wood from coming into direct contact with the snow and sticking to it. When you get home you will need to remove the wax before applying new tar.

Section 5
Touring in Norway

5.1 Norwegian mountain huts: DNT

Posted on 6 July 2006

DNT was formed in 1868 and since then has evolved into Norway's largest outdoor activity organisation. It has 207,000 members, about ten per cent of whom live outside Norway. The letters stand for Den Norske Turistforening. Until recently this was usually rendered as "The Norwegian Mountain Touring Association", but the preferred translation is now "The Norwegian Trekking Association". DNT acts as an environmental pressure group; it marks footpaths and ski routes; and it maintains a network of huts in remote areas.

Members can take advantage of budget accommodation at over 400 huts. Some are directly managed by DNT, but many more are run by local affiliates or private individuals. There are three categories of accommodation:

Staffed huts are similar in standard to the best Alpine huts or to large, rural youth hostels in Britain. Some have almost 200 beds. They have electricity and drying rooms. Some have showers and saunas and indoor toilets, but in others the toilets are in a separate block. Bunkrooms have two, four or more beds. You need a sheet sleeping bag, but in some huts the guardian will rent you one. A full meals service is provided, though in some staffed huts you have the option of preparing your own food in a members' kitchen. Many of the staffed huts only open for very short periods of the year, notably around Easter. At other times some of them have a small annexe that can be used on a self-service basis (see next paragraph). Though you can pay in cash, most staffed huts have Point of Sale machines for payment by credit or debit cards.

Self-service (provisioned) huts are smaller than staffed huts, usually sleeping from 5 to 25 people. There are bunk beds and blankets but you must take your own sheet sleeping bag. You make your own food, fetch water and tidy up afterwards. These huts are equipped with pots and pans, crockery and cutlery and they have supplies of dried and tinned food from which you help yourself. You pay by leaving cash in a secure box cemented into the wall or you can complete a direct debit single authorisation form and leave it in the secure box. These huts are locked, mainly using DNT's standard key which can be borrowed by members, usually against a cash deposit.

Unstaffed huts do not have food. Otherwise they are like the self-service huts.

It is not possible to reserve space at self-service or unstaffed huts. You just turn up. Depending on the time of year you may be the only people there, in which case it will take a while for the hut to warm up, for snow to melt for drinking water, etcetera. Alternatively the hut may already be very busy, in which case you may need to sleep on mattresses on the floor.

For current accommodation prices you should go to *www.dntoslo.no* then select the English-language version.

5.2 Troll Loipe

Posted on 16 June 2006

The Troll Loipe is a long-distance ski trail, about 170km in length. It runs alongside the eastern flank of the Gudbrandsdal valley, keeping mostly above 800 metres elevation and in parts reaching nearly 1200 metres. It starts in Høvringen and finishes in Lillehammer. The following notes are intended as an accurate summary of the route — but please be aware that things change from season to season and that some accommodation facilities may only be open in high season or at weekends.

In principle the Troll Loipe is marked with sticks along its entire length, at least during the period from 1 February until Easter. And in principle much of it is machine-prepared. In practice you need to be ready for off-track days, especially on the stages that are most distant from hotels. This gives the route a fair measure of challenge, and it calls for stamina and navigational skill.

Some people attempt the entire 170km while others split it into sections (Høvringen to Rondablikk and Høvringen to Venabu are the most obvious short versions).

Touring skis with metal edges are advised if you plan to do the whole route. Unusually for a linear tour ski hire is possible, through the hire shop in

Høvringen (Høvringen Skiskole). The owner is Henrik Morell, and by prior arrangement and at extra cost he will issue your skis at Høvringen and collect them from an agreed pickup spot on the E6 highway (eg Kvam, Ringebu, Lillehammer) after you have finished your tour. You can contact Henrik via *www.hoevringen-skiskole.com*.

Overnight stops

(For more details of accommodation between Høvringen and Venabu see Chapter 5.3.)

Høvringen can be reached by train from Oslo Sentral station. The rail line goes through Oslo Gardermoen airport. It is possible to leave un-needed kit at the left-luggage at Gardermoen or at Oslo Sentral Station. For train times go to Norwegian State Railway's website: *www.nsb.no*. You leave the train at Otta and do the final 23 km to Høvringen by taxi (stance outside the station; taxi fare about NOK 700).

Mysuseter. From Høvringen to Mysuseter is a stage of 20km. En route, about 6km from Høvringen, you pass Smuksjøseter Fjellstue, an isolated hotel.

Rondablikk. From Mysuseter this is a stage of just 10-15km, though you can lengthen the day by adding various loops.

Eldåbu. From Rondablikk this is a stage of 15km. Eldåbu is a DNT self-service hut with 18 beds.

Venabu. From Eldåbu this is a stage of 18km.

Øksendalen. From Venabu this is a stage of 25km. Accommodation is available in Friisvegen Turistsenter (*www.friisvegen.no*) at Måsåplassen. Alternatively there is a little self-service DNT hut about 5km before Øksendalen. It is called Jammersdalbu.

Vetåbu. From Øksendalen this is a stage of 22km. Vetåbu is a small DNT self-service hut.

Djupslia. From Vetåbu this is a stage of about 15km. Djupslia is a DNT self-service hut with 12 beds. Fifteen kilometres is too short for most skiers, and it is more usual to continue south and east to Hornsjø Høyfjellshotell (*www.hornsjoe.com*) a quirky old place that shares its site with a residential college for students of international development. That would give a stage of 38km from Vetåbu.

Alternatively, at about the same distance, you could try Pellestova, where the old Fjellstue has been refurbished and renamed Pellestova Hotell Hafjell. The website, at *www.pellestova.no*, is in Norwegian only.

Lillehammer. From Hornsjø this is a stage of 25-30 km, depending on whether you go via Nordseter or Sjusjøen. You need good snow conditions to ski all the way down to Lillehammer (and you need to be ready for some steep sections). You will end at Håkons Hall from where you can take a bus into the town centre. In Lillehammer there are several hotels, as well as a youth hostel which is described in Chapter 1.4.

5.3 Rondane

Posted on 10 September 2006

To the east of the Gudbrandsdal valley and about 300km north of Oslo, the Rondane National Park is a justifiably popular touring area. Access is fairly easy, by rail or Ekspressbus to Otta and then by taxi to mountain hotels. Or you can stay on the train to Hjerkinn, in the north, and start skiing from there. Skiers travelling by air can join northbound trains at Oslo Gardermoen airport.

In and around Rondane there is a good choice of accommodation of different types:

• Mountain hotels at Hjerkinn, Høvringen, Smuksjøseter, Mysuseter and Rondablikk. The hotel at Venabu, to the south of the range, is also very useful for north-south crossings.

• DNT staffed huts at Rondvassbu, Bjørnhollia and Grimsdalshytta. (These huts are usually only staffed for part of March and April, but you can use their self-service annexes at other times).

• Private staffed hut at Dorålseter.

• DNT self-service hut at Eldåbu.

There are several "standard" routes in Rondane.

Hjerkinn to Nesset is a crossing from northwest to southeast. The overnight stops are at Hjerkinn, Grimsdalshytta, Dorålseter, Rondvassbu, Bjørnhollia and then Nesset. Logistically this is tricky, for getting back to Oslo from Nesset is not straightforward. It is easier to turn south from Bjørnhollia, ski down to Eldåbu, and then either go west to Rondablikk or south to Venabu, in order to be within reach of the Oslo railway line again.

In its English-language programme of guided tours DNT sometimes offers a shorter north-south crossing. It starts from Høvringen then spends one night at Smuksjøseter before continuing to Rondvassbu, where two nights allow you a day's local skiing with a light pack. You then go to Eldåbu for a night before skiing out to Venabu.

Many skiers opt for circular tours, starting and finishing at Mysuseter. A fairly standard version would have the following overnights: Mysuseter, Smuksjøseter, Rondvassbu, Bjørnhollia, Eldåbu, Mysuseter. This itinerary, like the Hjerkinn to Nesset route, mostly follows valley routes, though you can in places go along the top of rounded ridges that run parallel to the standard valley-floor options.

If you really want to climb mountains then you can reach some of Rondane's tallest peaks if you base yourself at Rondvassbu. But these big mountains have ridges that are very steep and very narrow, and they are imprudent choices for the great majority of Nordic ski-tourers. There are better, more feasible, options to the south of Rondvassbu, and to the west of it; and possibly the best option for the bagger of rounded summits would be to have two or three days at Smuksjøseter and then two or three days at Rondvassbu.

Travel

The rail line from Oslo to Rondane goes through Oslo Gardermoen airport. It is possible to leave un-needed kit at the left-luggage there. For train times go to Norwegian State Railway's website: *www.nsb.no*.

Accommodation

Hjerkinn Fjellstue (*www.hjerkinn.no*) has a choice of twin rooms with ensuite shower and toilet and, in an annexe, dormitory accommodation.

There are several hotels in Høvringen. For details go to the local tourist office website (*www.hovringen.no*).

Smuksjøseter Fjellstue (*www.smuksjoseter.no*) is a little hotel in a marvellously wild location beside a frozen lake about 6km from Høvringen.

At Mysuseter there are two hotels: Mysuseter Fjellstue (*www.mysuseter.com*) and Rondane Spa Høyfjellshotell (*www.rondane.no*). Be aware that Mysuseter Fjellstue is sometimes fully booked in advance by tour operators.

Rondablikk Høyfjellshotell (*www.rondablikk.no*) is a large place with several different standards of accommodation.

At Venabu there are two hotels, Venabu Fjellhotell (*www.venabu.no*) and Gudbrandsdal Hotell Spidsbergseter (*www.sgh.no*).

DNT details and prices can be found at *www.turistforeningen.no* (or at *www.dntoslo.no*). Many of the hotels mentioned above will give a price reduction to DNT members.

Ski hire
Touring skis with metal edges can be rented from the hire shop in Høvringen (Høvringen Skiskole). The owner is Henrik Morell, and you can contact him via *www.hoevringen-skiskole.com*.

5.4 Finse Hut

Posted on 16 November 2006

Of all the DNT's huts, the one up at Finse is perhaps the best known among skiers who are based outside of Norway.

Partly this is because of its accessibility. Trains between Oslo and Bergen stop at Finse station, from where it is only 400 metres (on skis) to the hut itself.

Partly it is because it is at the meeting-point of two good but distinct touring areas: Hardangervidda and Skarvheimen.

And partly it is just because the Finse area has built up a reputation as a "must-see" place with all kinds of historical associations. Ernest Shackleton came to Finse in 1914 and camped on the glacier. (R. F. Scott didn't come when he was preparing for his own attempts on the South Pole, but there's a memorial to him here nonetheless.) Nansen came here. British royalty came here. Even Han Solo and Luke Skywalker came here — with Chewbacca — to shoot for *The Empire Strikes Back*, though they pretended it was the frozen planet Hoth.

Visitors seeking comfort can stay at the Finse 1222 Hotel just next to the station. (It's at 1222 metres elevation). But most skiers opt for the DNT hut, which is a big place with 150 beds, some in a large dormitory, others in small bunk-rooms.

It is usually staffed from mid-March to early May and provides a full meal service. There is a little shop at Reception that sells ski-waxes, confectionery, bottled beer and other essentials. (The local general store is contained within the Finse 1222 Hotel.)

Weather

You need to be careful up here. The website of the 1222 hotel carries this warning: "The climate and terrain at Finse are not suited for beginners. The arctic winter can be extremely tough and blizzards are common. Proper clothing, navigational equipment and experience are therefore necessary to enjoy the terrain around Finse without the company of a guide in the winter time."

I've stayed twice at Finse and on both occasions storms blew up suddenly. The first time, a gale-force whiteout (no exaggeration) turned the easy route to Hallingskeid hut into a scary epic. The second time, years later, after a still day on which we had been able to ski across the top of the nearby ice-cap, strong winds blew up. We retreated to Geilo to ski in the shelter of trees. But another party pressed on with their tour and were forced to dig a snowhole short of Krækkja hut.

If you are planning to tour (rather than to base yourself at the hut) it is therefore prudent to give yourself a couple of days at the hut to acclimatise, and to try to get an idea of the likely weather.

Ideas for day-tours

A good network of stick-marked routes converges on Finse. For example you can go southward to Appelsinhytta (an unlocked shelter close to a tongue of the Hardangerjøkul glacier). Or to the north you can go up towards Klemsbu, a little hut owned by Finse 1222 Hotel. (Ask at the hotel whether it will be open or locked). Another favourite day-tour goes north-east from Finse through the gorge called Kyrkjedøri (Church Door). Alternatively, if you want to take time out from touring and work on your downhill skills, then just to the north side of Finse station there is a little downhill ski centre with a drag lift.

Ideas for moving-along tours

Many first-time visitors spend a couple of nights at Finse and then ski roughly north-west to Hallingskeid Hut, a stage of about 20km over fairly flat ground. Hallingskeid is not staffed, but it's a nice hut and it makes a good base for a couple of days' local touring. From Hallingskeid you then go east, then north-east, to Geitrygghytta, which is a staffed hut that is usually open from early March through April. This stage is about 24km and involves climbing over a watershed at just over 1400m. You can spend a couple of days at Geitrygghytta, and have local day-tours. From Geitrygghytta you then go south back to Finse, either via Klemsbu (about 15km) or through Kyrkjedøri (about 20km).

If you prefer to tour southwards from Finse, on the Hardangervidda plateau, then a popular route would be via the huts at Kjeldebu (26km) and Krækkja (12km). From Krækkja you would either ski out to the railway line at Haugastøl or go (via Tuva hut) to the railway at Geilo.

5.5 More about Rondane

Posted on 2 April 2007

I spent last week leading a touring group in Rondane and based on that experience I'd like to add some further thoughts about the area.

First, here is an outline of what we did. We spent the first night at Mysuseter Fjellstue. Then we skied along the Troll Loipe to Smuksjøseter Fjellstue where we spent two nights; on the static day we climbed a rounded peak called Gråhøe (1751m). Then next day we skied along the old winter route past the rounded hill called Randen to the DNT hut at Rondvassbu. This route is no longer marked with sticks but there were plenty of tracks to follow so it is obviously still well-used.

From Rondvassbu we skied north along Rondvatn lake, and then climbed eastward to the watershed that divides Bergedalen valley from Langgluppdalen. We skied all the way down Langglupdalen, a wonderful descent that continued for fully 8 kilometres, and then came to a snowbound road that took us round to the DNT hut at Bjørnhollia.

After a night there we skied back to Rondvassbu, this time taking the shorter route along Illmanndalen valley. Next day we skied back down to Mysuseter: the tracks were quick and the 10 kilometres took just two hours so we had time after an early lunch to have a short tour on the fells just to the south of Mysuseter. (We climbed to the summit of Svinslåberge (1128m) and came down in a NNE direction, through a cluster of cabins and back down to the Troll Loipe, which took us back to Mysuseter where we spent the last night.)

We had warm, sunny conditions and cloudless skies for almost the whole week. There had been no fresh snowfall for at least a fortnight. This meant that we had to use klister or skins. As a result the first day, on the Troll Loipe, was harder work than it should have been. Also, the snow near Bjørnhollia was thin and patchy. The lowest kilometre of the Langglupdalen descent was a little fiddly as a result, and from there thin and icy snow made for a tedious slog on the last two kilometres along the (switchback) summer road. And then the first half hour next morning in Illmanndalen was also a bit tricky.

Otherwise it was a fine route through wonderful scenery and with good accommodation, and if I only had a week to spare I would do it again without changing anything.

However, if I had had more time I would have liked to stay longer at Rondvassbu. In the good conditions that we were enjoying it would have been possible to get up on to the Illmanhøe hills to the southeast of the hut. To the northwest we could have reached the nameless 1647m top above Rondvatn lake. And we could have made our way up into the high corries under Storsmeden summit. (A couple of English skiers were climbing the highest peaks, including Vinjeronden and Rondslottet, but they needed ice-axes and crampons.) Rondvassbu is a good hut, and like the other places we used it has hot showers, so it would be no hardship to spend a few extra days there.

Another night at Smuksjøseter Fjellstue would also have been nice, to give us the chance to ski over to Formokampen peak, to the south.

In spite of the warm and sunny weather, we had very good snow cover for most of the time. But it was obvious that the northern side of the Rondane mountains was experiencing much poorer conditions. From near the watershed that divides Bergedalen from Langgluppdalen we looked northwards to slopes that seemed almost completely devoid of snow. Touring parties on the classic route from Hjerkinn, via the huts at Grimsdalshytta and Dorålseter, were having a hard time of it. Two of our own party had done that route last winter, and they too had found it tough going, bad snow conditions causing them to make diversions that often ended in tedious and sometimes perilous bush-bashing. Maybe, in these days of climate change, that route is best kept for earlier in the season.

5.6 Touring in warm weather

Posted on 6 April 2007

It is Easter and in Scandinavia cross-country skiers are enjoying sunny, warm weather — and reasonable snow in spite of that. This time of year can bring great skiing, but it also throws up some unexpected risks and issues. Normally we plan for cold days, and we pack accordingly, pessimistically throwing in last-minute foul-weather items just before setting off for the airport. However, it pays to add a touch of optimism, too — don't forget how hot it can be. The following notes are based on a recent tour in Rondane.

Sunburn

The risk of sunburn is obvious enough, but don't forget your lips. On our tour I thought I was being careful, and frequently applied my usual lip-salve. But it wasn't good enough and for a week after I got home the scabs on my mouth made me look like I'd slept in a plate of porridge. Next time I'll take a very high-factor type.

Cuts and grazes

I skied mostly without gloves and it was fine, except on the occasions when I fell over and the hard grainy snow cut my hands. These were minor cuts, but I had more serious ones when, on arrival at one hut, I took off my skis and banged them into a drift of snow so that they would stand vertically. Unfortunately the "drift" was as hard as rock and the skis bounced off it, their metal edges gashing my fingers quite badly. Next day, in the mountains, we passed a Norwegian woman skier who was bandaging her hands; she too had cut them on her metal edges, whilst stopping to put on skins.

Blisters

Some of us suffered badly from blisters, and we got through a large supply of Compeed, micro-pore and padded Elastoplast. I think the problem was made worse than normal by hot, sweaty feet and by our heavy reliance on climbing skins, which lead unavoidably to a sort of choked stride. (We used the skins not just to climb hills but also to get up valleys; and sometimes we kept them on across flattish ground, rather than have the bother of applying klister.)

Klisters

Conditions were freeze-thaw, and for grip — except when using skins — we used klister (universal over a base layer of blue). Even with care our hands got sticky. To clean them we rubbed on sun cream or Nivea cream. We saw Norwegians using orange peel. They would eat the orange at breakfast and then save the peel until they waxed up. Had all else failed we would have used the little packets of margarine that were put out at breakfast.

Climbing skins

The tour took a heavy toll on our skins. One group member had both his skins fail, on consecutive days. So we had to do running repairs out on the snow. We used Araldite Rapid (good), duct tape (good) and electrician's tape (not so good).

Poles

The hard, crusty snow also took a toll on our poles and on the baskets especially. Our group had three baskets fail, all on Swix Mountain poles, which are usually bomb-proof. (In defence of Swix, they were all old poles that had seen a lot of service and not a lot of preventive maintenance.) We carried a spare telescopic pole, but group members preferred to do their own running repairs, with webbing straps and thin plastic tubing. Next time I'll take some spare Swix baskets.

Skis

Spring snow is abrasive and is hard on ski bases. Those in our group who had not glide-waxed before the tour were slower on the flat and also when going down hills, and seemed to get slower as the week went on.

A note about eye-care (From a posting on 27 May 2006)

The following is taken from a press release issued last winter by the Eyecare Trust, a registered charity (*www.eyecaretrust.org.uk*).

The Eyecare Trust today warned skiers and snowboarders of the risks of injuring their eyes on the slopes. Remarkably, the most common skiing injury is not to legs or arms — but to eyes!

The Eyecare Trust recommends spending time choosing the correct eyewear for the slopes. Expensive doesn't always mean best so follow the Trust's tips:

• Look for sunglasses or goggles that protect your eyes from UV light. The harmful rays to guard against are UVA and UVB. Seek out goggles and sunglasses that block at least 95 per cent of these rays.

• Choose the right lenses. Polycarbonate lenses cost slightly more but are highly resistant to shattering and filter out a large proportion of UV light without additional coatings.

• Select the right lens tint. Go for those that are yellow-orange or rose in hue. Sometimes, they are known as 'blue-blockers'. These colours will enhance contrast and will improve your vision, while also cutting out glare from the sun. Polarised lenses also filter out glare and reflected light.

5.7 Dave Leaning: Lindesnes to Nordkapp

Posted on 23 April 2008

For most of us in the UK the ski season is over, but for one British skier it will last another couple of weeks. He is Dave Leaning and he is nearing the end of an epic solo journey from Lindesnes to Nordkapp, from the most southerly point in Norway to the most northerly, a total distance of about 2500km. On the way he has maintained a blog, allowing friends and family to track his progress.

Aiming to follow a route that is fairly standard — that is, among the very small group of skiers that have attempted the end-to-end journey — he started on foot from Lindesnes just after midnight on 1 January 2008.

He walked the first 120km to Ljosland quickly, taking just four days. But then, as soon as he hit the snow, the troubles began. And the troubles have never really ended.

He started on skis from Ljosland, hauling a pulk on which he carried camping gear and several days' food. But he had to turn back after two days as the pulk proved too heavy in the deep, unconsolidated snow. To add to his problems he also had blisters from boots that were too tight.

And he had major difficulties in navigating, with his compass pointing erratically and almost at random, a problem that he eventually traced to "some clever mittens with a finger pocket which folded back to allow more dexterity with the fingers, this had a magnet to hold it back — no wonder the needle was all over the place."

Jettisoning the pulk, and the magnetic gloves, he restarted, now carrying a rucksack with only two days food, and headed north through the Setesdal mountains. He was delayed by a storm that kept him hut-bound at Sloaros for three days, but then pushed on to Haukeliseter where unexpectedly, and very touchingly, his father had turned up to meet him. (His father is John "Spud" Leaning, who is himself very well-known in the cross-country skiing community: he has served as Snowsport GB Nordic Director and as Chairman of the International Ski Federation Cross-Country Committee for Lowlanders.)

Haukeliseter is on the southern edge of Hardangervidda. And from here Dave's route should have gone northward over the 'Vidda to Finse. However, on 25 January he wrote: "Another massive setback — was all set to leave this morning and begin the long ski trek across the Hardanger plateau, when I found out that none of the cabins in between Haukeliseter and Finse will be open until late Feb. Without any possibility of shelter or resupply across this long stretch of wilderness I would have to carry at least 10 days' worth of rations in order to make it to Finse. The only way to do this would be to tow a pulk, and the snow conditions are such that this would be next to impossible for one man — or at least for this man"

This needs some clarification, for the huts on Hardangervidda are mainly unstaffed, just like the ones that Dave had used in Setesdal, and they are never really closed. Nevertheless, Dave decided not to ski across Hardangervidda, but instead to walk around it, using the road through Røldal to Odda and Tyssedal and onward to Eidfjord. From there he skied to Haugastøl, near Geilo, arriving on 30 January after a month of travel.

February was marked by more problems, the first of which was a shoulder injury, which made Dave choose not to ski north to Jotunheimen, as would be normal, but to walk on roads through Geilo towards Fagernes. (There was also a high risk of avalanche in Jotunheimen.)

From Hovda he was able to ski again and he moved on to Ringebu from where it should have been relatively easy going through Rondane, but he had a problem with his mobile phone that caused a long diversion — and more road walking. By the end of the month he was in Meraker, north of Røros.

In early March he twisted his ankle. This forced him to do more walking, rather than skiing. Then, when he did get back on skis, he broke his nose in a fall and sprained his wrist at the same time. But he pushed on doggedly, along the Kungsleden trail, finally reaching the Arctic Circle at the end of March, by now having covered about 2000km.

During April he has had to contend with the approach of spring, which makes rivers harder to cross. And then there has been toothache, requiring a detour to Kautokeino where a dentist extracted a wisdom tooth.

Through all these setbacks, Dave has kept moving with huge determination. (He is a Royal Marine Commando.) He is motivated largely by a wish to raise money for the charity MAG (the Mines Advisory Group) "which works in conflict zones around the world to clear landmines and dangerous unexploded ordnance, to enable people to escape from the poverty and suffering caused by conflict, and educate indigenous communities to lessen the threat of death and injury."

With a bit of luck — and it's surely time he had some — Dave should reach Nordkapp in another couple of weeks.

Footnote: Dave Leaning arrived at Nordkapp on 1 May. His overall journey duration was therefore 122 days. During the journey Dave posted frequent reports on a blog, but the site has now been taken down. However he has uploaded five videos to YouTube and they are still there. See www.youtube.com/user/skinorway08?feature=watch.

Fefor Høyfjellshotel

5.8 Peer Gynt Loipe

Posted on 30 March 2011

I'm just back from a busy week in Norway, in which one objective was to ski the Peer Gynt Loipe from Dalseter to Skeikampen. The distance is about 65km and I had wondered if I might manage it in a single day. I rang Grethe, who runs the hotel at Dalseter to ask if that was feasible.

"Yes," she said. "I know someone who did it in one day, a woman who used to run a hotel in Skeikampen."

"You mean Marie-Louise?" I asked, remembering our contact when *XCuk* featured holidays near there.

"No", Grethe said. "I mean Marie-Louise's mother."

Marie-Louise has seen enough of life to be showing a touch of grey. So I pictured her mum as a little old lady. If she could do it, I was at least in with a chance. This assumption of course harboured a flotilla of dodgy prejudices. And I'd suffer for them later.

Sharing our transfer bus from Oslo, I reached Dalseter at 21.00. After dinner there came a repack of the rucksack — heavy, for I planned more touring later in the week — a hopeful application of blue wax to my skis, and then bed.

Next morning I clipped into my skis at 05.30. It was still dark, but the track was easy for several kilometres and although I had a head torch I didn't use it. In spite of the hour it was warm and I soon had to rub on some red wax to get grip. The forecast threatened afternoon temperatures of plus five. If you have used waxable skis you'll appreciate that this was not — at all — a good prospect, so I was keen to cover as much distance as possible in the morning, and I worked hard at my kick and glide on the way to Hattdalsseter, a rustic collection of huts that I reached just as the sky was lightening.

It was good to be out on the snow. February had been busy with late bookings, as people who had been deferring their ski holiday realised they could defer no longer, and long office hours had been the result.

After maybe an hour I was over the high point near Hatdalsseter and skiing down to the flat land beyond. For no particular reason I thought of someone I once worked with. He was a regular enough guy, but when he sat down to write brochure copy something in his brain seemed to judder and his prose came out purple. I imagined he would be in his element here, now, as the sun lifted in glorious majesty over the rugged eastern hills and bestowed its gift of light upon the sparkling snowfields, while lofty Ruten peak wearing a mantle of ermine stood mute sentinel over the remote settlement of Lomseter, as if protecting its log-built cabins from some ancient, hideous troll.

Mind you it was undeniably a nice morning, and the loipe alongside Lomseter, which I had once unkindly described as the most boring piece of skiing in all Norway, now felt remote and northern. The usually scruffy huts, too, seemed somehow authentic and arctic — and if a costumed Lapp had leapt out and joikked at me it would have felt just right.

By 08.30 I was at the far end of the big lake in front of Fefor Høyfjellshotel, where a hundred years ago R. F. Scott had tested his preposterous motor sledges and where now the guests would be tucking into their porridge. I stopped to re-wax, hoping I could get away with one of the warmer tub waxes and avoid the hated klister.

As it turned out, the new wax was not quite right. But that didn't matter too much for I missed the intended gentle track to the Peer Gynt ski centre and instead found myself on the one that goes steeply down alongside the downhill piste. A parachute-job at the best of times, it was totally impossible with a heavy pack and I walked most of it, clipping back into my skis only for the final approach to the base-station cafe, in case anyone was watching. By now I had covered 30km and though it was only 10.00 it felt like time to stop for lunch.

Next to the cafe was a ski rental shop manned by a cheerful, bearded Viking and I went in to ask for his wax tip. Red, he said, possibly red-extra. I told him that was (or they were, for I had both of them on) what I was using — without joy — and I now wondered if it was time for klister. He said he was sure it was not.

I then offered to pay him to apply the grip-tape that I carried in case of emergency, which I now declared to be the state extant. I had never used it before and had warily listened to the reports of people who had. It seems to be the ski equivalent of Marmite: love it or hate it. The secret appears to lie in the length of tape applied, and I wanted a professional's judgement of that, rather than my own rough guess.

He agreed to do it, but just as he was about to start he decided to phone a friend, an expert in ski waxing, and the friend pronounced that it was now, after all, time for klister. So I bought a can of the new easy-on klister, applied some without effect, applied some more, again without success, then walked dejectedly most of the long loipe up to Gålå Høyfjellshotell, hoping I'd find better conditions at the higher altitude.

At Gålå the loipe network was a bit of a mess, and the art of signposting seemed to be in its infancy. At one downhill piste I lost the loipe altogether, until a helpful man told me I should walk for 300 metres up the piste and then I would find it again. Not intuitive.

But all the climbing at least improved the snow and I finally hit on a waxing strategy that kind of worked. Near Gålå Høyfjellshotell a Norwegian skier, struggling with the conditions, asked me what I was using. Universal klister plus red-extra wax, I said. He shook his head — this was a bridge too far — and went in to watch TV.

I pushed on along the track, the snow sucking at my skis like mud, still hoping to make Skeikampen by nightfall. But near the lovely little Fjellstue at Lauvåsen I experienced a catastrophic failure of energy system. It was now 15.00 and though I had covered only 45km I could go no further. The woman in charge of the Fjellstue gave me a basin of soup so large I could have navigated among the vegetables using compass bearings, and rented me a cosy log cabin, where the previous tenants had left some packet broth. I cooked it up and had three platefuls. Day of the soup.

Next morning I hoped to catch the 09.40 bus out of Skeikampen, so I was on the trail well before six. Four hours for 22km. I can walk quicker than that, so I expected to be down in the resort with time to spare. But the snow had frozen to boiler-plate in the night, and the easy-on klister was no good. Tube klister proved a little better, but only a little, and it took me over an hour to cover the undulating 7km to Fagerhøi. After that came a flatter stretch where I made better progress. But then the long descent to Skeikampen, which in mental rehearsal had been a breeze, was just too fast to ski. A hundred metres of schuss and I would have been up at Mach 2. The safe alternative was a quadriceps-burning half plough.

By 09.00 it was clear I had no chance of the early bus, so I took a break and then tried to savour the rest of the journey. I liked the Peer Gynt Loipe — nice track, nice scenery — and I hoped to do it again in future, though the next time I would schedule a stop at Lauvåsen. And I'd leave my heavy kit at Dalseter, and take buses back there via Lillehammer. Two days for this kind of distance would be challenging enough. One day was way too ambitious.

Down in Skeikampen I had a couple of hours before the next bus. So I went in to mooch a coffee from Marie-Louise. And told her how much I admired her mother.

Section 6
General Features

6.1 Skarverennet

Posted on 15 April 2007

The competitive XC ski season in Europe edges to a close next weekend with the running of Norway's *Skarverennet*, one of the largest cross-country ski races in the world.

Taking place on Saturday 21 April, the freestyle event will attract up to 14,000 entrants. Some will cover the full 38km course from Finse (Finse Hut pictured) to Ustaoset, near Geilo. Others will opt for the shorter (26km) stage from Haugastøl to Ustaoset. Many will be in the "recreational" class and will regard it as a kind of fun run, a last chance for a long day out on snow before the onset of spring. But others will be in the "competitor" class and will treat the event as a race — and some of them will treat it as a very serious race, for *Skarverennet* attracts the top Norwegian skiers.

Among the men taking part this year are Ole Einar Bjørndalen (last year's winner) and Frode Andresen and Kristen Skjelda, each of whom has won the event twice in the past. Among the women will be veteran Elin Nilsen, who has won the women's race thirteen times.

Inaugurated in 1974, *Skarverennet* takes place in Buskerud county and for much of its length it runs through Hallingskarvet National Park.

The full course, from Finse, is a challenging switchback. For the first six or seven kilometres you climb steadily, up from 1200 metres to around 1450 metres. Next the route undulates through spectacular high-mountain scenery — the escarpments of Hallingskarvet are on your left — until about six kilometres from the end. It then turns downhill and loses 300 metres of height on the way to Ustaoset, a fast finish that helps the winner achieve a time of about 1 hour and 20 minutes.

Skarverennet is very impressive logistically. There is no road access to Finse in winter, so all participants have to be taken to the start by rail. A total of ten trains will be needed, each with a capacity of about 1200 skiers (and their skis). Some trains will start as far away as Oslo, departing from Sentral Station at 05.30. But most will start from Geilo, which is where the majority of participants base themselves. The remoteness of the course calls for good safety and evacuation resources: one hundred snow-scooters will be stationed along the route and two helicopters will be kept on standby. To cope with track preparation, marshalling, manning drink stations and general operations a total of 1,000 volunteers will be needed; some will have been involved for many months.

The logistics are inevitably made more complex because the event takes place within a national park, and protection of the fragile environment has to be a prime concern.

Skarverennet is a very good example of how a "citizen" sporting event can bring important economic benefits to the community that hosts it. Over the race weekend a total of 30,000 people — participants and their families — stay in or around Geilo. It has been estimated that in 2006 they spent the equivalent of 4.5 million pounds sterling in connection with the race weekend. Of that, about 1.7 million pounds went on the race arrangements (track preparation, rail transport, safety, stewarding). The rest was general tourist expenditure, much of it spent in hotels, shops and bars, but with a large amount going to the temporary "Skarverenn Shop" which sells sporting goods. Geilo Sports Club (Geilo Idrettslag) netted a surplus of about 200,000 pounds. Some of this funded the club's three full-time employees, much of whose workload throughout the year is devoted to organising the race.

For more details of the event go to *www.skarverennet.no*.

6.2 How big is the British XC ski market?

Posted on 16 June 2007

I've been trying to find figures on the size of the UK cross-country ski market. But there is not much to go on. I have checked the websites of the sport's official bodies: SnowSport GB, SnowSport Scotland and SnowSport England (and its predecessor, ESC, the English Ski Council). But there is no solid statistical information. The best I can find is an ESC Nordic discussion paper written by Alan Jones which says, "It has been estimated that 1-2% of skiers in the UK participate in Nordic skiing, although no statistics have been published."

There was no statistical information available several years ago either — when I last searched. Back then, for a commercial reason, I was asked to come up with an estimate of the size of "the British market for overseas cross-country ski holidays".

I remember looking at tour operators' brochures to get an idea of the capacity that they were offering, and then checking their ATOL licence figures to see how much of that capacity they thought they might in fact sell. I then checked the brochures of the downhill operators to determine to what extent they were pushing the cross-country potential of their resorts. Armed with all this data I made the educated guess that each year about 20,000 overseas cross-country ski holidays would be taken by British residents. I wouldn't have bet the house on the accuracy of this estimate, but I had done my best with scant information, and I still think that the number was okay in a ballpark sort of way.

Recently I was talking about this with Paddy Field, who has been for many years a technical delegate for the International Ski Federation (FIS). And it turns out that about three years ago he was asked by FIS to assess the level of British participation in cross-country skiing. Paddy's remit was broader than mine. It was to estimate "the number of British people who would ski cross-country in an average year". That definition did include skiers taking foreign holidays, but it also embraced people who would ski in the British hills if and when the snow came, and also British military personnel who trained or raced on cross-country skis. Paddy's estimate, after a lot of searching and a lot of phone calls to people involved in the sport, was 50,000 people.

Two things emerge from our investigations. One is just how small a minority we are. Our estimated numbers are tiny in comparison with downhill skiing, which each year accounts for over a million holidays taken by British people.

The other is just how poor our knowledge is of the actual level of participation in our sport. Again the comparison with downhill skiing is instructive, for rates of British participation in downhill skiing have been measured carefully and in some detail for many years. There are two main sources of information.

The Ski Club of Great Britain's Snowsports Analysis

This is an independent investigation of the state of the UK snowsports market (which mainly means downhill skiing and snowboarding). The annual report is compiled using data from questionnaires sent to UK tour operators, resorts, travel agencies and transport companies during the season, alongside data from other industry reports.

The most recent report was published in October 2006 and related to winter 2005/2006. It estimated that the total UK snowsports market (the number of people taking a snowsports holiday) had reached 1.27 million people.

The report showed not only the total numbers travelling, but also the method of transportation to the resorts, the method of booking (through a tour operator or independently), the relative popularity of the various destination countries, the relative popularity of skiing and snowboarding and — for each of those disciplines — the proportions of beginner, intermediate and advanced participants. It also showed the relative proportion of men and women taking holidays (43% women).

The Ski Industry Report from Crystal Ski

This is the other main source of data. It amalgamates information from tour operators' own statistics, AC Nielson's TravelTrack market research, CAA published statistics, tourist office figures and travel agency feedback.

The 2006 report estimated that more than 1.15 million snowsport holidays were bought by British people in winter 2005/06. It also presented figures on the number of independent travellers, the number of passengers carried by low-frills airlines and regular scheduled airlines and the relative popularity of the different destination countries. It also measured the relative size and market share of the big ski tour operators.

Now I don't think it would be difficult to obtain similar information on cross-country skiing holidays. The number of relevant tour operators is small, so it would not be a huge task to contact everyone. Some of the bigger "relevant tour operators" are under the same ownership as the companies that already provide the figures used by the Ski Club and by Crystal, so the parent companies have already set a precedent for providing information.

A general reason why we need better figures is simple "corporate governance". Sports bodies are generally charged with increasing the level of participation in their sport. But how can they do this if they don't know the baseline?

A more specific reason is that the figures, if we had them, might cheer us all up. Both of the reports mentioned above show large and steady rises in the popularity of downhill skiing and snowboarding holidays. The Ski Club survey claimed a growth of 3 per cent on the previous year and a growth of 15 per cent since the start of the decade. The Crystal survey put the annual rise at 7 percent, and said that the number of ski holidays bought in 2005/06 is 40 per cent more than in the mid-80s, a period often regarded as the hey-day of British skiing. It is nice to think that cross-country skiing has shared in that growth. It would be even nicer to know for sure.

Footnote: Because of economic contraction the overall number of snowsport holidays bought by British people annually has now fallen well below one million.

6.3 London rollerski race

Posted on 4 August 2007

On Sunday 22 July over 50 rollerskiers took part in an afternoon of racing at Hillingdon Cycle Circuit, on the western outskirts of London and not too far from Heathrow airport. Thirty of them competed in a one-hour event and 21 in a 7.5 km race. For a minority sport like ours these are large numbers, and they point to the popularity of rollerskiing as an off-season activity.

One of the reasons for that popularity is the wide-open nature of the events in the racing calendar. They are open to all comers, and enthusiastic newcomers can find themselves sharing the field with very serious athletes preparing for high-level winter competition. The one-hour event at Hillingdon was a good example. Among the 30 participants, six were members of the British Development Squad. These were "junior" skiers (under 18) but they had a lot of experience and they were good. Last winter some of them had competed in top-level XC events in Norway and Austria — and had then gone on to take part in the European Youth Olympics in the Spanish Pyrenees. In the one-hour event two of them finished as sixth and seventh men (Simon Spencer and Andrew Musgrave) while one (Fiona Hughes) finished as second lady.

There were also some very experienced and very quick "seniors". For example the race winner was Carl Carrier, of the RAF, who has competed in biathlon at World Cup level. In second place came Mike Dixon, a contender in six Winter Olympic Games.

Further down the field, however, there were lots of "club-runners" — one or two of whom, like me, slowed things down considerably by opting to do classic technique on barrel-wheeled rollerskis. (The event was free-technique and the great majority of racers skated.)

The winner completed 21 circuits of the course in the hour, a total distance of just under 20 miles. Those of us at the other end of the spectrum logged nine circuits, or just over eight miles. This was judged a respectable enough tally by the very supportive spectators, and we were cheered and encouraged just as enthusiastically as the winners.

The racers came from far and wide. Members of the London Region Nordic Ski Club (LRNSC) were joined by skiers from cross-country ski clubs in Aviemore, Huntly, Lakeland, Manchester, Yorkshire and Wessex. There were also competitors from the Czech Republic, Russia and Germany

The popularity of events like these brings a lot of kudos to the clubs that host them. And so does the fact that such races count towards the British Roller Ski Series. But with the kudos there also comes a lot of organisational pressure, especially as regards the scoring. The one-hour event was a good example. The three LRNSC stalwarts in charge of scoring took up a strategic position near the top of the longest climb on the circuit (and therefore the slowest part of the course) and then spent a feverish hour trying to log every lap completed by every racer. It was very hard work for them, and it was made more so by the natural tendency of racers to come through in groups rather than one by one.

In a big athletics meeting the organisers will control numbers by having heats. In a major XC marathon on snow the organisers will often have a "trim-class" for fun-runners whose time will not be strictly monitored and might not be recorded at all. British rollerski racing may need to come up with such stratagems if numbers get any bigger.

In the meantime, the LRNSC scorers will be looking forward with some trepidation to their annual four-hour event in October. It usually attracts about forty racers, and the quickest of them can cover 70 miles in the four hours. That's a lot of laps to count…

For details of events in the London area see *www.londonnordic.org.uk*.

Footnote: LRNSC now has digital lap-timing equipment.

6.4 Cross-country skiing for blind people

Posted on 18 January 2008

On our New Year week at Dalseter, in Norway, we shared the hotel with a group of blind and partially sighted skiers and their sighted guides. They had come up from Denmark on a trip organised by *Dansk Blindesamfund*. This was their first visit to Dalseter. In previous years they had stayed in Sjusjøen, at Sjusjøen Fjellstue. But now that the Fjellstue is being converted from a hotel to an apartment complex, they needed to try somewhere new.

They seemed to enjoy Dalseter. One of their guides told us that they liked the straightforward layout of the hotel. Because all the rooms are in one building — there is no annexe — and because the main floors have a similar floor plan, the place is easy to get to know. The more confident of the blind guests were therefore able to find their way around alone after just a short time.

The skiing seemed to suit them too. Most days we would pass some or all of them on the tracks just north of the hotel. Most skied in classic technique, letting the tracks do some of the steering for them. But a few skated — on the Peer Gynt Loipe that links Dalseter to Fefor. One of the skaters was a former Paralympic athlete and he was exceptionally quick.

In such groups the arrangement is that for each blind skier there is at least one sighted guide. Often a group will contain more sighted guides than blind skiers, to allow the guides some free time. Out on the snow, the guide skis ahead of the blind skier and constantly relays information about the track and terrain. (To help communication, the Danish guides wore nifty microphone headsets that connected to little amplified speakers on their bumbags.)

From time to time you will encounter visually impaired British skiers out on tracks in the Alps or Scandinavia. Mainly they will be on trips organised by Vitalise, which was formerly known as the Guide Dogs for the Blind Association. This winter, for example, they have an early-April week in Arctic Finland, based in Ylläs.

Just like the Danish group at Dalseter, Vitalise groups rely heavily on the services of sighted guides. The guides are unpaid volunteers who receive a subsidised holiday in return for their work.

The nature of that work depends on the level of experience of the blind skiers. If they already have good skiing experience then the guide's task is mainly to "see" the upcoming ground for them and to tell them what to expect. But if the skiers are complete beginners then of course the task also includes the teaching of skills. And for that the guide needs to be a very good instructor who really understands how basic techniques are made up.

An instructor working with sighted clients will rely heavily on giving demonstrations, on showing how techniques should be performed and then asking the students to copy what they have seen. With blind skiers the instructor can't do that. Instead he or she has to be able to deconstruct a technique into its component parts, to describe each part clearly, and then to identify and correct faults.

It's hard work, as the guides themselves will tell you. But most of them will also be able to tell you an inspiring tale or two, to help you understand why they do it. I like the one about the visually impaired beginner on her first morning at Sjusjøen. The guide walked with her out on to the frozen lake, helped her clip into her skis and said "Okay, you can set off in any direction you choose." The skier burst into tears. When she had regained some composure she said, "It's the first time in my whole life that I've had that kind of choice."

Footnote: In January 2013 Vitalise "ceased its Vitalise Holidays service". However, some of its former sighted guides continue to run holidays on a relatively informal basis, occasionally recruiting new guides from cross-country ski clubs.

6.5 Norway in January

Posted on 10 February 2008

In late January I skied in Norway with an *XCuk* group. I was surprised by how many other British skiers were in Norway at the same time.

Our group went to Høvringen. Also traveling with *XCuk* were two people going to Nordseter. Sharing our flights to Oslo on 26 January were other British skiers bound for Venabu and for Vinstra. In total there were about fifty British cross-country skiers arriving in Oslo ——on what was by normal Norwegian standards a very low-season date.

And it was not only British skiers that were heading for the snows. In the middle of our week a group of 35 German cross-country skiers arrived at Putten Seter, a cabin settlement 6km from Høvringen.

Other northern countries are also seeing a growth in January business. Arctic Finland is increasingly featured by the larger downhill ski operators, who run charter flights throughout the entire winter and offer bargain prices in low season. Some cross-country skiers are either booking a downhill package holiday, but not taking the ski equipment or lift-pass options, or they are buying "flight-only" and arranging their own accommodation.

Similar changes in skiing habits have happened before. For example, in the early 1990s most British cross-country skiers going to the Alps would travel only at Christmas/New Year or in February. January seemed impossibly cold and dark and tour operators considered it too difficult to sell. Now a January trip to the Alps appears quite ordinary and natural.

Conditions in January

During our week we had very good snow, more than a metre deep. Daily breakfast-time air temperatures were: minus 8, minus 7, plus 2, minus 11, minus 6, minus 6. We skied mainly on blue-extra wax, but we also used some green on the coldest day and some violet and red on the warmest day.

One day was stormy and we stayed close to base, spending the morning on the hotel's nursery downhill piste and the afternoon on a nearby forest loipe. Otherwise we ranged far and wide, covering 110 kilometres in the week. This included an unsuccessful off-track attempt at a 1500m peak and a successful off-track attempt at a 1400m one (Formokampen, on a clear and sunny day). Had we been there later in the season I doubt we would have done any more.

Early-season drawbacks

The main problem in the early season — colder weather apart — is that not all the skiing "infrastructure" will be in operation.

This means a shortage of places to get into, to shelter from the cold. It suited us to return to our hotel at lunchtime on a couple of days. But otherwise we wanted to stay out all day, and in that respect we were limited by the small choice of available cafés. There were two in which the owners were in residence (Putten Seter and Smuksjøseter) but neither was officially open to the public. In the event we were allowed into both to eat our sandwiches, but we never knew until we got there whether the door would be open or locked. If we hadn't been allowed in, our entire holiday experience would have been a lot less pleasant. (We carried a nylon group shelter and happily used it once on a windy hillside, but it won't ever take the place of a café selling hot chocolate.)

Another drawback is that not all the tracks will be regularly cut.

A relatively minor irritation in the early season, when daylight hours are limited, is that Norwegian mountain hotels tend to serve breakfast quite late, from 08.00 or 08.30. We got into the habit of nipping across to the ski-room at 07.30 and preparing our skis before breakfast. We would then be ready to start skiing at 09.30. On some days we stayed out until the daylight faded, which — if the weather was clear — was at about 17.00.

6.6 Off-track skiing

Posted on 3 January 2009

With *XCuk's* booking season well advanced, we are able to see some trends. One is that we're attracting a lot of off-track skiers. It's not a new trend — we attracted a lot last season, and the season before that. This winter, 25 per cent of people who have booked with us have chosen centre-based off-track skiing.

It suggests, frankly, that there are many people who can't find what they want in the programmes of other holiday companies. And that, I think, is a hangover from the changes that have affected off-track skiing since the 1980s.

In the early 1980s if you joined an off-track holiday you would expect your companions to want long days on the snow, touring over mixed terrain with moderate hills. Okay, you'd expect them to enjoy the thrill of skiing down those hills, but it wasn't the main aim. The main aim was simply to experience and enjoy wild countryside in winter conditions.

Then around the mid-1980s there came a change. Originating mainly in the USA there developed a new emphasis on skiing steep ground, the steeper the better. The recently-revived Telemark turn was picked up by expert skiers, who experimented with it and re-tuned it. They wanted to make it faster and to give it a shorter radius, and for this they introduced Alpine style skis — short fat boards with soft camber and immense turning capability.

Such skis called for stiffer boots, increasingly made from plastic. And the steep ground called for heavier bindings, with release plates that added further to the weight. Back-country skiers of this type were no longer content with (or equipped for) meandering over mixed terrain. They wanted to ski the fall-line.

And that was fair enough. Skiing is a broad church and there is room for many denominations. But problems did arise when this new type of back-country skier joined a group of the more traditional off-track skiers.

The first problem was that the "new" skiers owned climbing skins while the "traditionalists" did not. So the new skiers would get up the hills more quickly. This caused the group to spread out — a headache for the party leader. The tour organisers' response was to make skins mandatory. However this caused bigger problems because now all party members could climb steeper and longer slopes — but some of them didn't have the skill or hardware for getting back down. Unless the leader was extra vigilant the group would scatter alarmingly over the mountainside.

The upshot was that some skiers became wary of booking off-track holidays, and some leaders refused to lead them. And the tour operators became wary of organising them. In the 2003/4 brochure of Waymark Holidays, at that time the UK's leading cross-country specialist, there were five off-track resorts: four in Norway and one in Switzerland. In the current Waymark programme, now operated by Exodus Travels, there is only one.

The "new" skiers seem to have found a niche with other specialist operators and clubs. The "traditionalists", as I say, are coming increasingly to us. And we are keen to attract them. Even for our highest grade off-track holidays we say "We don't mind how you get down the hills — you can traverse and kick-turn or ski the fall-line — but we want you to be able to get down fairly quickly, so that the other members of the party are not kept waiting."

We've had people tell us that this talk of traversing and kick-turning sounds old-fashioned, and that we risk alienating mainstream off-track skiers. But as far as we are concerned we are in the mainstream. In the three years since we set up the company I've skied a lot in Norway, often off-track. Sometimes I've toured between DNT huts, where everyone leaves their skis outside and their boots in the porch, which makes it easy to see who is using what. In three years I have seen just one pair of plastic boots at a hut, on a German woman using alpine ski-mountaineering kit. And hers were the only Alpine-cambered skis I have seen at huts. My other off-track skiing has involved day-tours from hotels, and on these trips I have seen just one small handful of skiers using plastic boots and soft skis. They were a British group. And, since their routes were relatively easy, they would have fared better on lighter kit.

6.7 Fefor and Scott

Posted on 10 February 2009

I'm just back from Norway, where I was instructing on our *Back to Basics* course at Dalseter. On several days we skied along the Peer Gynt Loipe and came within a few kilometres of the mountain hotel at Fefor. For people from the UK, Fefor is closely linked with Robert Falcon Scott (of the Antarctic) and that link will become even closer in the next twelve months, as the area gets ready to commemorate the 100th anniversary of the explorer's visit.

Scott came to Fefor in March 1910, while preparing for the ill-fated Terra Nova expedition, his second expedition to the South. His specific project in Norway was to continue testing the caterpillar-tracked motor sledges that the Wolseley Motor Company had supplied. Scott hoped they would help in the eventual push for the Pole, complementing the efforts of ponies and dogs.

However the Fefor programme got off to a bad start when the test vehicle almost immediately broke an axle — even though it had already coped with snowy surfaces in France. The axle was mended by the blacksmith down in the village of Vinstra, and Scott persisted in his confident view that such teething problems would be resolved.

Unfortunately his confidence turned out to be misplaced. Less than a week after the Terra Nova reached base camp in the McMurdo Sound, in January 1911, one of the expedition's three motor sledges broke through the sea ice and was irrecoverably lost. At about the same time, Scott was writing of the other two: "The motor sledges are working well, but not very well; the small difficulties will be got over, but I rather fear they will never draw the loads we expect of them. Still they promise to be a help, and they are a lively and attractive feature of our present scene as they drone along over the floe."

In fact when they were put to the test on the Southern Journey to the Pole, which started in November 1911, they lasted only three and four days respectively before they broke down and had to be abandoned (thus managing just a tiny proportion of a journey that was to go on until the following March).

By November 1911 some of Scott's men had lost all faith in the motor sledges, and quite a lot of faith in their leader. In his diary, Oates (who was in charge of the ponies) recalled grumbling at this time to Meares (who was in charge of the dogs): "We both damned the motors. 3 motors at £1,000 each, 19 ponies at £5 each, 32 dogs at 30/- each. If Scott fails to get to the Pole he jolly well deserves it." Another member, Lashly, expressed something close to relief when the motor sledges finally gave out, saying that their very frequent breakdowns had caused him such a lot of hard physical work that actually man-hauling the sledge loads could not be any more tiring.

The centenary of the Fefor visit will no doubt re-open the old debates about Scott's leadership, for his decisions about transportation have always been controversial, to say the least. This relates not just to the motor sledges, but also to Scott's preference for ponies as beasts of burden, rather than dogs.

But the debates can range far beyond methods of transport, and far beyond the relative strengths of Scott and Amundsen, the Norwegian who got to the Pole first. Even without the benefit of duty-free alcohol they can spiral off into rants about the decline of the British Empire. The stiff-upper-lippishness of Scott, a British naval captain apparently incapable of decisive action, can be portrayed as a sign of decadence in the entire British establishment. (Amundsen, correspondingly, can be seen as the expression of a confident and emerging Norwegian nationalism.)

Such debates can go on for hours. So if you just want to ski — rather than sit up all night having the kind of rows you haven't had since you were a student — then Fefor, next March, is best avoided. But I expect we'll have it in the brochure all the same.

6.8 Karen Darke

Posted 10 March 2009

A lecture tour is under way in the UK and the presenter is a woman who, though normally confined to a wheelchair, has successfully completed a traverse of the Greenland ice cap using a specially designed sit-ski.

The woman is Karen Darke, who fell while rock-climbing on a sea cliff near Aberdeen in 1993, when she was 21. The accident left her paralysed from the chest down, though she still has the use of her arms.

"Just the night before my accident," she writes on her website "I said I would rather die than be paralysed, but little did I know what lay ahead. Instead I found fortune in my misfortune, inspiration from people in similar and more challenging situations all around me, and began pursuing alternative ways to access the outdoors."

Now aged 37, Karen has completed many challenges. In 1997 she crossed the Tien Shan and Karakoram mountains of Central Asia on a handbike. Then in 2000 came a handbike tour along the length of the Japanese archipelago. The year 2003 brought a 1200-mile sea kayak journey off the coasts of Canada and Alaska. Then in 2006 came two major projects.

One was a crossing of the Indian Himalaya by handbike. And the other was the Greenland expedition, which was completed in May 2006, and which involved an unsupported 600-kilometre traverse of the ice cap. Accompanied by a team of five able-bodied skiers, Karen started near Tasilaq on the east coast and finished in Kangerlussuaq on the west. The journey took 29 days.

Being disabled, Karen faced major challenges in coping with conditions in Greenland. With great frankness her website talks about these. Here's an example:

"I put catheters in the freezer, along with bladder wash solutions ... If you're worried about leaks, then do everything you can to avoid them. I taped all the connections together between my catheter/bag etc. with zinc oxide tape to make sure nothing popped off, and I reinforced bits of my catheter bag I know are vulnerable to bursting, with the same tape, and duct tape on top!"

You can read a lot more such detail on her website, at *www.karendarke.com*.

Karen has written an autobiography, called *If you fall . . .* You can order a signed copy from her website for £10 (post free in the UK). Or you can find it on Amazon.

The book was written before the Greenland trip was undertaken and therefore does not cover it. But it may not be long before a second volume of autobiography is needed. Karen has plans for a ski expedition in Antarctica, including an attempt on the South Pole. Another goal is to make the British handbike team for the London Paralympics in 2012.

Footnote: Karen Darke's second book was published in September 2012. It is called Boundless: An adventure beyond limits. You can buy it through her website. A Kindle version is available through Amazon. You can "look inside" the Kindle version and read the first two chapters, one of which tells how the idea of the Greenland crossing came about.

Karen's partner, Andy Kirkpatrick, who was one of the Greenland team, has posted a short video about the expedition on Youtube. It has music but no commentary. It is at: www.youtube.com/watch?v=81KTqJ-3bR0

On Karen's website there is a long article about the Greenland expedition.

During the London Paralympic Games in September 2012 Karen won a silver medal in the handbike event.

6.9 In Memoriam Waymark Holidays

Posted on 20 May 2007

On 27 April 2007, just three weeks ago, the British tour operator Waymark Holidays vacated its offices in Slough, Berkshire. Nominally the company relocated to Balham, southwest London, in a move that its website insisted everyone was "very excited about". But only a couple of the staff actually made the move to Balham. The others left or were made redundant.

Understandably, the move is being presented in a brave-faced sort of way as a strategic and progressive merger between Waymark and its sister company Exodus Travels. But it is difficult to refute the claim that Waymark is being swallowed. There will be no more Waymark brochures. Instead, some holidays and courses will still retain the Waymark name, but they will only appear within Exodus brochures.

It's a sad end to a good little company, a company that was in many ways synonymous with British recreational cross-country skiing. It seemed that everyone who had tried XC skiing had travelled at least once with Waymark. The company set a standard. Describing a new area that they had discovered you would hear people say, "The level of difficulty is about Waymark grade 3/4" — and everyone would know exactly what they meant.

Waymark Holidays was founded in late 1973, by two people, Noel Vincent and Peggy Hounslow, who had previously worked for Ramblers Holidays. Already up in years when Ramblers decided to move their office out of London, Peggy and Vincent (he hated being called Noel) took retirement rather than relocate. Soon, however, they tired of inactivity and set up the new company. They were supported in the project by a former Ramblers leader, Ruth Chamberlain, and by Ruth's husband Humfrey, a man whose success in other businesses gave him the resources to guarantee the CAA bond. He joined Peggy and Vincent on the board of the new company.

Initially an operator of walking holidays, Waymark — as I understand it — got into cross-country skiing after an approach by Rod Tuck, an ex-Marine who had founded Kvitåvatn Fjellstoge in the Telemark region of Norway. From these beginnings the winter business grew steadily until at its peak the company carried over 2,000 XC clients each winter, more than half of them to Norway.

A trawl through the three decades of Waymark brochures is like a course in the social history of XC skiing. At the broadest level, for example, you can see the effects of climate change: even in the early 1990s, in the Alps, there were still resorts as low as 600 metres, something that would be unthinkable now. You can see the ebb and flow of airlines and routes: DanAir into Berne, AirUK into Innsbruck. At the higher end of the grades you can see a steady rise in technical difficulty, as the increased use of climbing skins and soft-cambered carving skis took groups on to more and more serious terrain (notably in Santa Maria and Kühtai) — a process in which the boundary between Nordic touring and ski-mountaineering seemed almost to disappear.

For the last five years, both Waymark and Exodus have been owned by First Choice plc, a major holiday firm. Ever since it became involved in the Activity-Adventure sector, First Choice has appeared to be content to make room in its portfolio for companies that compete with one another. For example, the board seemed to take a relaxed view of the fact that both Exodus and Waymark offered similar XC skiing holidays, and even of the fact that they did so in neighbouring resorts, a situation that in other large organisations might have provoked rationalisation and cost-cutting.

If the "Wexodus" merger is a sign of a general change of strategy, then it will be interesting to see what happens next. First Choice itself has recently announced that it plans to merge with TUI, a move that will create a huge multinational corporation with a global reach. As TUI already owns the tour operator Headwater, which is another fairly large player in the British XC holiday market, we can perhaps expect further rationalisation.

6.10 Navigation — lost in thought

Posted on 27 July 2008

Teaching navigation is one of those ideal, balanced-life occupations that combine healthy physical activity and intellectual challenge. In the UK, in summer, I instruct and assess at the National Navigation Award Scheme's bronze and silver levels, and at both levels my job is to take students on long country walks and watch how they work things out mentally. And then I try to help them work things out better. It can be fascinating.

At bronze level the students are taught basic skills, and then they are assessed on terrain that is generally straightforward. The navigational sectors mainly consist of single stages: any student who can confidently and consistently get from A to B will earn a pass. But even at this level, although the actual map-reading skills are quite basic, it is easy to distinguish strong navigators from weaker ones. The strong navigators will be, in an overall way, much more switched on mentally and much more aware of their surroundings.

They will constantly examine the ground for confirmation of position, and will always be mentally ticking off large and small features as they go past them. And they will have an open mind about how the features shown on the map will actually appear on the ground — a stream might be a torrent or a trickle, a field boundary might be a sturdy wall or a badly eroded ditch-mound. The weaker students, by contrast, will be fixated by the map itself, and may simply fail to recognize the majority of the features on the ground.

At silver level the navigation is trickier. A larger set of skills is required, the paths are less well defined and the target features are less obvious. And the stages are more complex. It is no longer just a matter of getting from A to B. Now the students have to get from A to D, and on the way they must call in at both B and C.

It is quite challenging, and sometimes the students get it wrong.

The stronger and weaker navigators will respond differently to getting it wrong.

The stronger students will say, "Sorry, but I've messed this up. I'm going to go back to the start and work it out again."

The weaker students will hold tenaciously to the belief that they are right, even though Reality strongly suggests otherwise. They have been aiming for a bridge over a stream, let's say, but when they have used map and compass to find the direction and then walked on the bearing for the calculated amount of time, they fail to come to a bridge. Even worse, there is no stream in sight. Nevertheless, they are adamant that they have come to the right spot.

It is then the job of the instructor to give them a hard time.

"So where's the bridge?"

"Well, obviously there is no bridge, and I think the map is wrong."

"And how about the stream that is shown on the map – where is that?"

"As I say, I think the map is wrong. Maybe there once was a stream here, but your map is an old one and the stream must have dried up."

This kind of exchange can go on for a long time, for there are many potential sources of error that are — importantly — not the fault of the navigator. Maps can indeed be wrongly drawn. Streams can indeed dry up. Changes in land-use can alter the landscape. Compasses can be faulty. The underlying rock can be magnetic.

But, much more commonly, navigators can simply get it wrong. And their understandable reluctance to admit their mistake often leads to what psychologists call "cognitive dissonance". This term refers to what happens when a person holds two conflicting beliefs at the same time, and tries to bring them into a sort of harmony by modifying one of them.

Belief Number One (*I have navigated correctly*) can be brought into harmony with Belief Number Two (*But I don't seem to be in the right place*) if you modify Belief Number Two by adding the comment: *The map is therefore wrong.*

This is a very common sort of error and I've seen it, and committed it, lots of times. Most memorably, coming off Ben Starav one winter's day a group of us convinced ourselves that the map was ridiculously badly drawn — until a clearing of the mist showed that the ill-drawn river below us was incontrovertibly a wide inlet of the sea and we had come down the wrong side of the mountain.

The lesson is: you've got to be open — always — to the possibility that you are wrong. Even if you have a good grasp of navigational techniques you can still make mistakes. And mistakes can start to reveal themselves in small, undramatic ways. Ground and map will begin to seem just a little inconsistent and your mind will try to resolve those inconsistencies by supplying you, subtly, with new assumptions about what is happening. An expected road-crossing doesn't come on schedule so you assume it must have been the path-crossing you encountered five minutes ago. You then start to go downhill more steeply than expected, so you assume the map is badly drawn. And so on, until you are quite seriously off-route.

As I said, it is fascinating. The interplay of technical skills and mental processes is continuous and intricate. And if I stop a student who is struggling over a difficult sector and ask them to make explicit all their assumptions as to where we are and how we got here, then the discussion can get quite cerebral.

"Hey! This is cosmology! This is Zen and the art of land navigation!" a student joked during a recent course.

It was hardly that.

All the same, if Karrimor ever starts to make purple robes in Goretex — I'm having one.

> Due to volcanic activity on Iceland, Oslo Airport is temporarily closed for traffic.

6.11 Long way home from the snow

Posted on 28 April 2010

The world of British cross-country skiing is a small one, but even so I was surprised by how many people knew we got caught up in the travel disruption caused by the Icelandic volcano. Thanks for your emails wishing us luck in our journey home.

When the volcano erupted we were in Kvitåvatn in Norway on a family-holiday-come-business-planning trip. Fortunately all our *XCuk* clients had by this time returned home, and initially we were quite relaxed about the eruption, feeling that the dust would soon blow away. But as the week wore on we realised that our flight — on the Sunday — would probably not operate. So we returned to Oslo airport a day early in our hire car and, to cut a very long story short, drove it for 2000 kilometres to Paris Charles de Gaulle airport, which was as close to the UK as the rental company would let us take it.

It took us the best part of three days to get home from Oslo, including a few hours sightseeing in the sun at Sacre Coeur in Paris while we waited for the train to Calais. In Calais itself we joined a large crowd of displaced people on the night ferry to Dover. On the ship's tannoy the captain welcomed us as "the refugees" and if we'd been greeted at the English dock by Winston Churchill it would have felt just right.

As it was we were met by my father-in-law, whose car — normally the quintessence of reliability — broke down twice on what should have been a two-hour drive but in fact took six. In both cases the RAC came out and fixed us up.

Few events have no redeeming features and one positive side-effect of the journey is that our nine-year-old son's life-long travel sickness has now well and truly disappeared. About 24 hours into the journey he was asking if we could do more of this kind of thing, and suggested that Pakistan would make an interesting overland destination.

Volcanic disasters are about as one-off as it's possible to be. So it's probably pointless to draw lessons from the recent disruption. But should we ever again be faced with a similar situation we will be armed with the following prejudices:

1) Transport companies will react very, very slowly. Days will pass before train, bus and ferry providers realise that there is a large new demand for their services. On their website they will tell you to ring their help line for the latest information. The help line will however connect you to an answering machine — which will advise you to go to the website for the latest details.

2) Designated information desks at airports will probably be utterly useless. At Oslo airport on the Saturday, having learned that our flight the following day had now been cancelled, we were told to come back on Tuesday.

"Why Tuesday?"

"Well, they think things will be better by Tuesday."

"Why will things be better by Tuesday?"

"Well, we don't know, but that's what they are saying."

"But who are they, who are saying this?"

"The people on the TV."

At Paris airport there was an information desk staffed by two people.

"We are trying to get back to England. Can you give us any advice about how to do that?"

"Sorry, but the airspace is closed and we have no information about ground transport. Try the SNCF rail terminus at the other end of the building."

"But the car rental people have just told us that the railway workers are on strike."

"Sorry, we have no information about that."

"Do you know about buses?"

"Sorry, we have no information about that. You would need to go into Paris and check there."

"But how do we get into Paris if the railways are on strike?"

"Sorry . . ."

Finally they directed us to a pay-for-use internet machine, which turned out to be broken.

We decided that the best course was to find something — anything — that was moving and get on it. So we took the RER metro into Paris then booked a train ticket from the Gare du Nord to Calais, in the hope that as foot passengers we would fairly easily get on to a ferry. (The trains were in fact working to schedule and we saw no sign of a railway strike.)

3) Getting home costs a *lot* of money.

6.12 Online applications for XC skiers

Posted on 8 January 2012

If you are one of the many people who pack a laptop, netbook or smart phone when you go on a skiing holiday, you've probably already found some web sites that carry ski-related content. To add to your list, here are some that I have found useful.

Skisporet

Skisporet ("The ski track") is a GPS-based system that shows the state of track-preparation at individual ski resorts within Norway. At present there are about 140 resorts in the system, and in each of them the track-cutting machines are fitted with GPS devices.

Every 20 seconds the GPS sends a signal by satellite to a host computer. This tracks the position of the machine and displays its progress on a topographical map. From the map you can see which tracks have been prepared, and when they were last prepared.

Skisporet is presented only in Norwegian and if you are not familiar with that language the best way to start is to go to the homepage at *www.skisporet.no*. There you will see a map of the whole of Norway, with lots of little squares superimposed upon it. Each square represents a ski "resort" — Sjusjøen or Espedalen, for example.

The individual squares are in different colours, and these show when track-preparation was last carried out:

Light green means 0-3 hours ago ("Timer" is the Norwegian word for "hours")

Orange means 3-6 hours ago

Blue means 12-48 hours ago

Red means 2-30 days ago ("Dager" is the Norwegian word for "days")

Black means 30 or more days ago.

You can use the zoom tool for a closer view of the region that interests you. If you hover on any square, the name of the resort it represents will be displayed.

If you click on one of the squares you will go to the page for that resort and can then see the detailed situation, with all the tracks displayed on a map. The same colour-coding applies, so you can tell when each individual loipe was last cut.

You will also see, on the resort map, black and white circles. These represent the individual loipe-machines, and if you click on them they will give some details about the current position of the machines. I've just been looking at one of them and saw the following details:

Oppdatert 6 timer siden — means updated 6 hours ago

Status Stanset — means its status is stationery

Hastighet 0 km/t — means that its speed is 0 km per hour

Kompasskurs Ukjent — means that its compass course is unknown

Hoyde over havet 871 meter — means that it is at 871 metres above sea-level

Eies / driftes av Sjusjøen — means that it is owned or managed by Sjusjøen

At some resorts the loipe-machine may also be used for preparing downhill slopes or clearing car parks, so be ready for the occasional odd reading. Also, be aware that some resorts may sometimes use snowscooters to prepare the narrower tracks; the snowscooters might not be fitted with GPS.

Yr.no

Yr.no is a very good weather-forecasting site. It is in Norwegian but there is a (partial) English version. For regions or specific locations you can see short and long-term forecasts. They are updated two or three times a day. They show temperature, wind-strength and direction and likely amounts of precipitation. (Precipitation is measured in millimetres of water, not snow. So if the forecast is for one millimetre of precipitation, you could get between one and three centimetres of snow.)

The site is at *www.yr.no*.

Swix Wax Wizard

Maintained by the Norwegian ski-wax manufacturer, this site helps you choose the appropriate wax-of-the-day for your skis. You can use it to choose grip wax or glide wax. First you need to specify what standard of skier you are: Pro, Sport or Recreational. Then you input details of air-temperature, humidity and snow-type.

For example, if you are a recreational skier and it's minus five Celsius and the snow is quite new, the wizard will tell you to use *blue-extra* grip wax.

Okay, most of us would have gotten there on our own, but the application becomes more helpful at warmer temperatures. To try this, choose a trickier temperature: plus one degree Celsius, say. If you specify new snow the wizard will recommend *red special*. But if you specify old snow it will recommend *red silver*. And if you then specify corn snow (wet snow that has gone through several freeze-thaw cycles) it will recommend *universal klister*. If you have ever tried to wax skis for temperatures above zero, you will know the value of such advice.

The wizard is hidden away in the "swixschool" website and the quickest way to get to it is simply to enter "swix wax wizard" in your search engine.

It will be interesting to see how such applications develop and multiply in the future, particularly as the technologies converge. For example, if GPS transmission and smart phones were to come together, that could deliver inexpensive personal tracking devices that might save the lives of lost or injured skiers.

Section 7
Fitness Training

7.1 Fitness tests

Posted on 29 October 2007

The clocks have gone back. Temperatures in Scandinavia are edging towards zero. So it's time to think more seriously about our readiness for the coming ski season, and perhaps to test our fitness, to see how we have progressed in the last few months and to judge how much work still has to be done.

You can make up your own tests, like walking or running a lap of your local park and recording your time on a regular basis. However you can also choose from a wide range of fitness tests that have been validated against the general population and therefore show you how you compare with the general population.

Tests can be good motivators for individuals, and they are also useful for coaches who want to encourage their students to improve — and want to be able to show them evidence of improvement.

Tests can be static or dynamic.

STATIC TESTS are mainly concerned with measuring body composition and resting heart rate.

Body composition — body mass index

Body Mass Index (BMI) is an approximate measure of whether your weight is within a healthy range. You calculate it by dividing your weight in kilos by your height in metres, and then dividing the result again by your height in metres.

So, if you weigh 80 kg and you are 1.75 metres tall, then your BMI is 26.1.

The World Health Organisation has set the following norms for BMI scores:

- Under 18.4 = Underweight
- Between 18.5 and 24.9 = Ideal
- Between 25 and 29.9 = Overweight
- Between 30 and 39.9 = Obese
- Over 40 = Very obese

BMI is a fairly rough and ready indicator. It is not suitable for athletes or body builders (who would give "false readings" because they have a lot of muscle, and because muscle is heavier than fat). Nevertheless, it's a useful measure for ordinary people who want a general guide to whether they need to lose weight, and if so how much.

Body composition — percentage body fat

This is a better measure of body composition than BMI, but — unless you have a friend who knows how to use skin-fold callipers — it requires a bio-electrical impedance device. Professional-quality models cost over £200 but you can buy cheaper (and rather less accurate) versions on the High Street.

Average levels of body fat are 18-25% for men, and 25-30% for women. However, athletes will have much lower levels: 6-13% for men and 14-20% for women.

Body composition — waist: hip ratio

To calculate your waist: hip ratio you first measure your waist at the narrowest part, usually at the navel, after a normal exhalation. Then you measure your hips at their widest part. Then you divide your waist size by your hip size to obtain the ratio. A figure higher than 0.95 (men) or 0.80 (women) is a sign that you are overweight.

For men, a waist circumference over 94cm (37 inches) is in itself an indication of higher risk of health problems. For women the figure is over 80cm (32 inches).

Resting heart rate

For this you take your pulse when sitting or lying down, ideally first thing in the morning before you have eaten or drunk anything.

A rate of about 68 beats per minute or less (for men) or about 72 or less for women is generally considered to be good for ordinary people. Athletes will have much lower rates — elite athletes perhaps as low as 45.

DYNAMIC tests require you to perform a physical activity at maximal or near maximal effort. Whereas people of any level of fitness can safely do the static tests, the dynamic ones can be stressful and you need to be careful. If in doubt, take medical advice before doing them.

Rockport walking test

This test of aerobic fitness was developed at University of Massachusetts and is described at: *www.exrx.net/Calculators/Rockport.html*.

Using a heart-rate monitor you record your pre-test and post-test pulse rates. Using a stop-watch you record your time to walk one mile at best-effort pace. You then feed the data, together with your age and weight, into an online calculator, which sorts your results into one of five fitness categories. As a bonus, you are given a fitness programme based on your score.

This is a really useful test for Nordic walking instructors wanting to introduce a bit of variety and structured challenge into their classes.

Sharkey 1.5 mile running test

This test of aerobic fitness was developed by Dr Brian Sharkey. An exercise scientist who worked with the US cross-country ski team, he correlated field results to lab tests and set out general norms.

The test requires you to run at best effort pace for 1.5 miles and record your time. Average times are about 12 minutes for men and 13 minutes for women. It is described at *www.exrx.net/Calculators/OneAndHalf.html*.

Shuttle runs

These are tests of speed-endurance. The best-known is the Bleep (or Beep) Test, in which you run back and forward on a 20-metre track, trying to keep in time with a pre-recorded "bleep" signal whose frequency gets faster as the test goes on. You can buy DVDs or MP3 downloads with recordings of the bleeps.

A less structured version of the test is the sort of shuttle run that Tim Henman used during his tennis career. With this you set up a course of 20 metres, then run from one end to the other and back, seeing how many times you can do it in a minute. After a rest of a minute you repeat the test, and then again after another rest of one minute.

Whichever tests you choose, you should use them regularly but infrequently. The idea is that they should motivate you to make gradual and steady improvements in your performance. Avoid the real temptation to repeat them obsessively every few days, or you'll wear yourself out.

7.2 The Training Year: Base Training — Endurance

Posted on 14 June 2008

It's only June. But if we were elite ski-racers we would be well into our annual training programme by now. We would have taken a month off at the end of the season just gone, and for that month we would have abandoned formal training in favour of a relaxed programme of active recovery. We would have used activities like hill-walking, cycling or kayaking to keep our bodies working, but in a fun sort of way.

And then we would have started structured training again. By now we would be in the base-training phase, working mainly to develop our aerobic capacity and our general strength. Our purpose would be to build a good foundation that would sustain more intense workouts later in the year.

We are not elite ski racers, but even so we can do ourselves a lot of good by following their example — up to a point. Base training is important for everybody, irrespective of current level of fitness.

The thinking behind base training is very well expressed in Rob Sleamaker's book *Serious Training for Endurance Athletes*, first written in 1989 and now, in its second edition, something of a classic.

The idea, Sleamaker says, is to "construct an intricate and effective aerobic foundation and plumbing system". This construction project involves not just heart and lungs, but also the entire vascular system (capillaries as well as arteries and veins). It also involves the aerobic energy system, which includes the ability of the body to burn fat at low exercise intensity.

It is a big job to build these systems up, and it needs a lot of time and attention. Elite ski racers will approach it with dedication. At the very top of the scale, they will train for perhaps 800 hours a year (the Norwegian Olympic hero Bjørn Dæhlie apparently did 1000 hours) and a significant proportion of that time will be devoted to base training.

And if that sounds like bad news, the good news is that base training should not feel like hard work. Sleamaker recommends that as much as 60-70% of all activity in this phase should be carried out at low intensity. This means a level that feels easy, that allows you to hold a conversation while on the move, and at which your heart-rate remains at 60-70% of your maximum value. At this intensity you should be able to keep going for an hour or more.

So, to get yourself ready for the winter, take yourself out and do some long, slow distance. For most of us that will mean cycling or country walking or Nordic walking. For some it will mean gentle running. But do keep it gentle and be sure to keep your heart rate in the correct zone. You will help yourself by using a heart-rate monitor.

As a quick and rough guide to determining the correct heart rate, subtract your age in years from the number 220. This gives your "maximum heart rate". For low intensity training keep your heart rate down to 60-70 per cent of your maximum. (So, if you are aged 50, your "maximum" will be 220 minus 50, or 170 beats per minute. Sixty per cent of that is 102 and seventy per cent is 119.)

Sleamaker suggests that, for endurance athletes in general, the base-training phase should last for the first four months of the training year. For cross-country skiers this means roughly the months of May, June, July and August. Thereafter the training should move into an "intense" phase, where intensity levels are increased to help prepare for the upcoming competitive season.

But, remember, this applies to competitive athletes. For the rest of us there may be little point in moving to a very intense second level. If our main aim is just to improve our general readiness for the ski season we can make the base phase longer, and then maybe go to a *slightly* more intense level, in which we do slightly less of the long, slow distance and instead substitute some intervals and speed work.

7.3 The Training Year: Base Training — Strength

Posted on 21 June 2008

In the previous posting we said that during the base-training phase we should do some regular strength conditioning as well as the aerobic endurance work. Part of the rationale is to increase the amount of force you can generate with each movement, so that when skiing you get more glide for each kick or pole-push. But another purpose is to strengthen the muscles, tendons and other connective tissue — to help avoid the risk of injury.

Once again a good resource is Rob Sleamaker's book *Serious Training for Endurance Athletes*. He sets out guidelines for the amount, type and intensity of the strength training.

Amount: He suggests that during the base phase you should devote 20 per cent of your total training hours to strength training.

Type: He says that, in general, strength training exercises should target the muscles employed in the sport for which you are training. But he adds "During the base phase, however, it is less critical to be completely sport-specific in strength exercises."

Intensity: He recommends "a high-repetition, low-to-moderate resistance method for all strength training." This should involve 12-20 repetitions per set, with 30-60 seconds between sets. When a set of 20 starts to feel easy, you should increase the resistance.

Sleamaker lists strength exercises that are specifically useful for XC skiers:

- Wide-stance squats
- Leg extensions
- Leg curls
- Seated rowing
- Lat pull-down
- Hip abduction/adduction
- Abdominal crunches
- Bent-knee sit-ups (to work abdominals)
- Lower-leg raises
- Back hyperextensions
- Bench press
- Sitting military press

Another good source for strength conditioning is Bill Pearl's book, *Getting Stronger — Weight Training for Sports*. It is a comprehensive guide to training with machines and free weights, and it has a useful section devoted to cross-country skiing, with exercises for the "off-season", the "pre-season" and the "in-season" periods. Once again the recommendation for the base phase is light loads and high reps. Favoured exercises are:

- Barbell squats
- Leg extensions
- Leg curls
- Seated rowing
- Lat pull-down
- Hip abduction/adduction using cables
- Lying leg cross-over (to work abdominals)
- Barbell upright rowing
- Side leg raises with cable
- Dumbbell pullover
- Push-downs on a lat machine

If you compare this list with Sleamaker's list you'll see that it is — reassuringly — very similar. There is broad agreement as to what kinds of exercises give a good preparation for cross-country skiing.

7.4 The Training Year: Base Training — Speed

Posted on 30 June 2008

There are many variants of speed work. The most common are intervals, *fartlek* and pyramids. All three are good for increasing your basic pace, allowing you to go faster for longer periods. The following examples use walking as the activity, but you can adapt for jogging, cycling or other endurance activities.

Interval Training

In interval training, bursts of high-intensity effort are alternated with periods of active recovery.

Short-distance interval work can be done, for example, around the perimeter of football pitches. A simple routine would involve walking one side of the pitch slowly, then one side at moderate pace, then the third side slowly, and then the fourth side at moderate pace. The number of circuits of the pitch can be increased as your fitness develops.

To give variety to short-distance sessions, and to increase the intensity, you can work on a pattern of reducing-recovery intervals. Using a square field whose sides are each 150 metres long, the sequence might now look like this:

- walk slowly round all four 150-metre sides to warm up
- do one side fast, one side slow
- do one side fast then do a shorter side, say 140-metres, slow
- do one side fast then do a still shorter side, say 130-metres, slow
- continue to reduce the recovery interval by a fixed amount each time.

Longer-distance interval training is particularly useful for people training for endurance events. The most straightforward way to proceed is to find a park with one long side. Simply walk along it in one direction at a slow pace, and then turn and walk back at a fast pace, repeating the sequence several times.

Fartlek

Interval training requires that regular bursts of speed are alternated with regular recovery periods. For a less structured alternative you can try *fartlek*, a Swedish word that means "speed play" and denotes an irregular mix of work and active recovery. On a country route you might walk slowly down the lane to the bridge, then go more quickly up the hill to the farmhouse, then slowly along until you reach the forest, then go really quickly to the far forest boundary. You just make it up as you go along.

Pyramids

In pyramid training you gradually increase the intensity of effort until you reach a peak, and then gradually decrease the intensity until you are back at your starting level. If you were to draw a graph of this, it would be shaped like a pyramid.

For a good example take a look at Simon Waterson's book *Commando Workout* (Thorsons, 2002). It describes a 30-minute routine for power walkers or joggers. Suggesting that you do it almost every day, Waterson says that this is how commandos keep themselves aerobically fit. The routine is perhaps unlikely to fulfil his publisher's promise of "total fitness in 4 weeks" but it's useful for days when you want an intensive workout. It is also a good way, if the weather is too poor to train outdoors, to make a treadmill session interesting, which is always something of challenge.

You start with 5 minutes at Waterson's "Level 3" (equivalent to gentle walking) then progress as follows:

- 2.5 minutes at Level 5 (moderate intensity; you can hold a conversation)
- 2.5 minutes at Level 6 (breathing heavily; conversation is more difficult)
- 2.5 minutes at Level 7 (feels like hard work)
- 2.5 minutes at Level 8 (harder still)
- 2.5 minutes at Level 9 (almost maximum effort)

Then you descend back to Level 6 at the same rate at which you ascended, taking 2.5 minutes at each of the levels. You then warm down for 5 minutes at Level 3.

Waterson has designed the workout so that it fits into a 30-minute slot. But you can adapt it to suit your own requirements. Personally I prefer a 60-minute workout, with longer warm-up and warm-down periods, so when I do this kind of training I start with 15 minutes of low (but increasing) intensity, then move up and down the pyramid, then finish with 15 minutes of low (and slowly decreasing) intensity.

Speed work should form only a small part of your total training time. During the base training phase elite athletes will devote only about 10 per cent of their total training time to speed and interval training. For the rest of us an even smaller amount will be appropriate.

7.5 Training for older skiers

Posted on 7 September 2008

British people who go cross-country skiing tend to be somewhat older than the general population. This raises issues about how they should prepare physically for their skiing holiday. And these issues link interestingly to more general considerations about coping with the process of growing older.

Broadly speaking there are two ways of looking at the relationship between ageing and fitness: a gloomy one and a more optimistic one.

The gloomy one implies that from a very early age, perhaps as early as 20, life is a gradual process of decline in physical ability. Unhappily, there is a lot of evidence to support this view. Here are some examples.

Muscle mass has been found to decline from about age 30. This affects muscle endurance, strength and power.

Basal metabolic rate also declines, from the age of 20, at a rate of one or two per cent per decade. This is said to be one of the reasons behind "middle-age spread" — your body needs less energy for basic functioning, so unless you reduce your dietary intake your weight will increase.

Aerobic endurance — stamina — also declines. One summary (Griffin: see footnote) says: "Maximal aerobic capacity decreases in both men and women, with an average decline of about 10 per cent per decade between the ages of 25-65." Related to this, maximum heart rate reduces each decade by 5 to 10 beats per minute.

There is also a decline in the efficiency of the lungs. The volume of air that a seventy year-old can breathe in may be only half of what a thirty year-old can manage.

To this already long list you can add that bone density reduces, capillary density reduces, flexibility reduces and balance skills decline. Not an especially cheering prospect.

The more optimistic view acknowledges all the changes just described, but says they are partly the result of the more sedentary lifestyle that older people adopt, rather than of the ageing process itself. Okay, they accept there is an unavoidable degree of physiological decline, but they argue that it is only really limiting if you are an elite athlete. The rest of us — who have never reached our physical potential — can still keep improving. We just need to work hard at it.

The optimists also point out that our ideas have changed as to the optimum age for endurance athletes. Fifty years ago the accepted wisdom was that they reach their peak at about 20. Now the view is that they need years of training to build their aerobic endurance, and today the target age for peak performance is closer to 30.

Other optimistic data comes frequently from "masters" ski races — competitive events for veteran skiers. Consider the results of the 30km classic technique event at the 2008 Masters World Cup in Idaho. The fastest man in the 55-59 years category, the oldest category for that race, finished in 1 hr 26 mins. In the youngest age-category, 30–34 years, the winner finished in the slightly slower time of 1 hr 32 mins.

An even more remarkable story from Idaho concerns Russian competitor Lev Litvinov, whose age put him in the 85-99 years category. On March 1 he finished the 10km classic race in 50 minutes, fully 30 minutes ahead of the second-fastest finisher in the category. Just to show it wasn't a fluke he was out on skis again on March 6, and won his age-group in the 15km classic race in a time of 1 hr 16 minutes, this time beating the second-fastest by 47 minutes.

The optimists conclude that, given good health, we can be very fit at almost any age. But we need to keep training, and as we get older we need to train a little bit harder.

Our training needs to include endurance work to maintain cardio-vascular efficiency. But to counter the possible decline of muscle mass we should also do some strength work, ideally two or three times a week. The best place for that is the gym, with a structured programme of resistance training using relatively heavy weights. But if you are irrevocably gym-phobic you can put together some circuit training routines to do at home. Exercises like press-ups, tricep dips and squats are useful and require no equipment. You can help yourself further by buying a pair of dumbbells and using them to train the muscles of your arms, shoulders, chest and back.

One group of British skiers who will right now be working on strength and stamina are those who have booked on our Engadin Ski Marathon course in March. Most of them, like the instructor, are over 50. All of them will hope for personal best times. None of them will give a damn how old they are.

Footnote. The reference on page 106 is to: Griffin, Sue (2006). Training the Over 50s. A&C Black. London.

7.6 Light on your skis

Posted on 19 January 2009

It's mid-January and the gym where I work as a personal trainer is buzzing with New Year's resolutions, most of them involving weight loss. Here is a selection of the weight-management advice we offer to our members, which I present now on the assumption (I may be totally wrong) that many skiers will have made similar resolutions.

We recommend tackling the problem through a combination of aerobic exercise, strength training, diet, and various other ways of raising the body's metabolic rate.

Aerobic exercise

Aerobic exercise is the main choice of most overweight gym users, and it's a good choice. Machines like treadmills, cross-trainers, rowers, steppers and bikes are all effective ways to expend energy and burn fat. It is however important to train at the right intensity, and we encourage members to work within training zones based on their heart rates. (See Chapter 7.2 for the arithmetic.)

If a member is seriously out of condition we advise them to take things slowly and to work at a steady pace, for example to walk on a treadmill at a consistent 3mph for about 30 minutes (after warming up). This will give them a calorie burn of around 150 kcals for the 30 minutes. And it will also raise their metabolic rate for a few hours after the workout, in an afterburn effect in which the body uses more than the usual amount of energy.

However with a fitter member we often recommend some form of interval or pyramid training. This might still involve walking on a treadmill, but now the member might alternate 5-minute periods at 3.5mph with 2-minute periods at 4mph. (The actual speeds and durations are determined by looking at the fitness of the individual, but we generally aim at a spread of about 60-80 per cent of their maximum heart rate.)

With interval training, the "fast" speed is set higher than the individual's usual steady pace, and this makes it more intense than steady-pace training — so the calorie burn is usually higher. An additional and important benefit is that the afterburn is more intense than with steady-pace training, and it also lasts much longer, up to 18 hours.

We also recommend that members do a daily short workout at home before breakfast, mainly to increase their metabolic rate.

Resistance training

Muscle tissue is — metabolically — very active, much more so than fat. So the more muscle you build, the more calories you will use even when resting. The rule of thumb is that for every pound of muscle you gain, your body will use 50 extra calories per day.

Many gym users know this already. And they have also read that regular resistance training can raise basal metabolic rates by up to 15 per cent. So they are not opposed to the idea of using resistance machines or even free weights.

But they are often surprised to learn that for resistance training to be effective it needs to feel like hard work. Left to their own devices many will happily knock out 50 repetitions on a machine set at a very low resistance, with almost no benefit. As a general rule we try get them to perform three sets of 10 reps, with the resistance heavy enough to cause fatigue by the last two reps. (So, if they were to continue beyond 10 reps they could maybe manage 12, but not 20.) We recommend they progress by increasing the rep count gradually, over a few weeks, to 15. Then they should increase the weight and reduce the rep count back to 10.

Diet

Most people seem to have a fair idea, in principle, of what constitutes a good diet — the woman who had four croissants every day for breakfast was a notable exception — and we don't get involved in the detail of their diet unless asked. But we do recommend that they use a food diary and record all intake of food and drink for at least a week. We give them the choice to approach it on a "usual-behaviour" or "best-behaviour" basis. If they opt for "usual-behaviour" they will often be galvanized into action when they see the number of naughty treats ingested, or when they see the unbalanced scheduling of their food intake — very commonly a pattern of miserly breakfasts and lunches and then heavy dinners late in the evening. If they opt instead for "best-behaviour" they may lose a couple of pounds during the week that they are recording, which is very motivating.

Boosting basal metabolic rate

Your body uses a lot of energy simply in staying alive. Your basal metabolic rate — the amount of energy you expend even if you just lie in bed all day — can be about 60 per cent of your total daily requirement. So anything you can do to boost your basal rate is worth considering. Here are some effective examples:

- Drinking plenty of water
- Pre-breakfast workouts
- Drinking green tea
- Eating little and often
- Eating spicy food
- Turning down your central heating. The body has to work harder to stay warm.
- Having a sauna. Again the body has to work hard to regulate its temperature.

7.7 A cross-country skier's guide to choosing a gym

Posted on 4 July 2009

With UK temperatures at record highs it might seem strange to be thinking of gyms. But summer isn't just a good time to work on your pre-season fitness. It's also a good time to pick up a gym membership bargain. In many gyms summer is a slack period and special offers are much more likely now than at other times of year.

As well as discounted rates for full-year memberships, some gyms offer short-term deals in summer, typically for six or eight weeks. They are targeted at people involved in the education system but usually they are also made available to the wider public.

If you are thinking of joining a gym, keep in the very front of your mind that the fitness industry is massively big business. Recently I read that "the value of the UK health and fitness clubs market is said to be about £4 billion". Big business is seldom squeamish about evaluating its customers in a cold-blooded sort of way. So don't be bashful about evaluating your local gyms in the same spirit. A year's membership can cost several hundred pounds or more, so it makes sense to spend your money wisely.

Ask each of your local gyms for a week's free guest pass. And then go along to each of them at the time you would normally expect to train. This is especially important if your normal training time will be in the early evening. Many gyms are fairly quiet up until about six and are then frantically busy until about eight-thirty. You want to see — before committing yourself to a membership — just how busy your gym is.

If you do take a guest pass, be ready to receive a telephone call a couple of weeks later, from a member of the sales staff trying to convert you into a full member. Rehearse beforehand your response to that call.

PRICE CONSIDERATIONS

Does the price of membership reflect the going rate for your area?

Are there any hidden costs? For example there may be in-vogue kit such as vibration plates ("Power Plate"), for which there is an extra charge.

What is the minimum membership period? In many gyms you will be committed for a minimum of one year. Some gyms are rigidly inflexible over this. Others will be more accommodating and will for example freeze your membership for a few weeks if you are ill or injured or out of the country.

Be wary of any gym that seems unwilling to tell you frankly and upfront just what its prices are. If the sales people stubbornly refuse to disclose their prices over the phone but instead say, "Come in and talk to us about the package you need", then you can expect to meet with some very hard selling when you do visit. By all means go and see them, but be sure to rehearse in advance your getaway speech — "Thanks. I now need to think about it all." And be ready for that getaway speech to be met in turn by a "really special offer" that might include a couple of free months added on to your first year's membership. So, you should have a second-phase getaway speech. Rehearse it in advance. And leave your credit card at home.

THINGS TO LOOK FOR IN A GYM

General facilities

Is there ample free car-parking, even at peak times?

Is there safe bicycle-parking?

Is there good security — both for you and for your personal belongings?

Are there any restricted times — at which the gym, or some part of it, is reserved for women only, or for children or for a local sports club?

Is the music (and its volume) to your taste?

Are any classes (such circuit training, spinning, boxercise, yoga, etc.) available at the times when you are likely to train?

Is there a swimming pool? (If the gym does have classes and a pool — but you don't plan to use them — bear in mind that you will be paying for them anyway, for they will be reflected in the price of your membership. So you might find better value in a more simple gym.)

Is the gym clean? Is it well-ventilated with good temperature control?

Is any merchandise or food/drink supplementation offered for sale? If so, are the gym staff members excessively pushy with it?

Other members

Are kids allowed to use the gym? If so, at what times? And what is the age-limit?

Is the gym frequented by bodybuilders? Many bodybuilders are gentle souls motivated by ideals of human beauty that go back to the time of ancient Greece. But others, following a shorter tradition that dates merely from Arnold Schwarzenegger's bodybuilding heyday, are much less civil. They will repeatedly crash the weights and try to persuade the staff to flood the entire gym with very loud rock music. Check out what sort frequents your gym — and think about whether you can co-exist with them.

Equipment

Is there a good variety of equipment? The keen XC skier needs a very wide range of kit. Make sure there is a choice of cardio machines (treadmills, bicycles, cross-trainers, steppers, arm cycles, rowing machines). You'll also need fixed-plane resistance machines targeting all the main muscle groups (leg press, leg curl and extension, chest press, shoulder press, lat pulldown, abdominal curl). And if you are already an experienced gym user you will appreciate a good selection of free weights as well. Cable-machines are useful, too, as are matted areas on which you can use Swiss balls and medicine balls.

As well as the variety of equipment, make sure that there is a sufficient amount of it, especially at peak hours. You don't want to have to queue to get on a machine. And once you are on it, you don't want to feel pressured to get off just because someone else is waiting.

Try to ascertain whether the equipment is well looked after. How much kit is "out of order" at any one time? How quickly is broken kit repaired? As for the equipment that is in service, are there any minor faults, such as malfunctioning TV monitors, ripped seats on machines, missing pedal straps on bicycles? Do you get the impression that anybody is trying to sort these problems? Don't be shy about asking other gym users for their views about the standard of maintenance.

Staff

Are the personnel friendly, qualified, knowledgeable, helpful? Make sure that they are *really* helpful. Many gyms have computer systems that record the number of "interactions" with members, and it is a sad fact that the staff can use them in a token sort of way, and may be reluctant to get involved in interactions that involve anything more than saying hello.

Tell an instructor that you are thinking about a cross-country skiing holiday and ask for some advice about how to train for it. If they don't have a clue, be worried. If they don't have a clue but immediately suggest you sign up for a course of personal training at a cost of several hundred pounds, be deeply worried.

Are inductions given by qualified staff? Was your own induction simply a tour round the machines during which you were shown basic operational procedures, like how to switch on a treadmill and make it go faster? Or was it enriched by some guidance as to how hard and how often you should train on the treadmill (and on a good selection of other kit)?

Are one-to-one sessions included in the cost of your membership (to help you design a training programme and then review it)?

Is any "testing" offered (body-fat monitoring, etc.)? Some gyms do this free of charge. Others, notably those that are moving towards a "wellness" approach (rather than a "fitness" one) may offer a range of health and fitness tests for which they will charge premium rates.

In summary, treat a gym membership as a very important purchase, and make your decisions only after a lot of thought.

7.8 Prehab for skiers

Posted on 13 February 2010

One of the perks of being a tour operator is that I get more than my fair share of skiing. The flip-side is that I've come to expect more than my fair share of injuries. They're mostly bumps and bruises and the occasional muscle strain, rather than anything serious, but I try to minimise them nevertheless — not just by skiing prudently but by including some strengthening exercises in my pre-season training. I touched on this a few weeks ago in a posting about biomechanics. (See Chapter 9.5.)

I've found that a useful way to think about injury prevention is via the concept of "prehabilitation" or prehab. The idea behind prehab is that you can avoid many of the most common injuries in skiing (or in any other sport) by targeted physical training. Like many useful concepts it's open to various definitions, and these range from the general to the specific.

General prehab

In one version the word prehabilitation is used in a very general way, almost as a synonym for "prevention". And that broad kind of approach is — definitely — applicable to XC skiing. For example, many ski injuries occur as a result of tiredness. So, if you can build up your cardiovascular and muscular endurance in a general way it will help keep you whole.

To quote from personal experience, last season I was victim to skier's thumb and to mild concussion. Both conditions resulted from falls when I was stationary or almost stationary. The thumb incident happened while I was talking to another skier in an icy area and my skis just slipped from under me. The concussion incident, a couple of days later, happened after I had taken my skis off and was walking into a cafe for lunch. I slipped on ice at the doorway, couldn't get my hands up to protect myself in time, and head-butted the door-post.

Both incidents seemed at the time to fall into the "just one of those things" category. But I don't think they would have happened if I had been feeling fresher and more alert. The previous week, with a group of fit and experienced track skiers, I had covered 150km on quite hilly terrain and it had left me just a little weary.

And so, with that in mind, this year I've upped my pre-season training volume to 10 hours a week. And I've upped the intensity, too, mainly forsaking Nordic walking for road runs and moderately hard gym workouts.

Another example of a general approach to prehabilitation might focus on bodily stiffness. Many of us lack flexibility, from too sedentary a lifestyle and too much time hunched over computers. And the stiffness makes us ski badly and fall over. In that context, a programme of mobilisation and stretching, to increase flexibility, could be seen as a general form of injury prevention.

Body imbalance prehab

In a less general version, prehabilitation can refer to a training approach that focuses on body imbalances. If you have a recurring lower-back problem, for example, it may be caused by tight hamstrings — in which case a programme of stretching could help you. Turning that around, a proactive trainer might say: if you have tight hamstrings, let's do something about it *before* you get a bad back. In this version of prehabilitation you avoid injuries by identifying body imbalances and remedying them. It's quite a specialised business, usually the province of physiotherapists and specially qualified personal trainers, and is not generally suitable for a DIY approach.

Specific prehab

A third and much more specific version of prehabilitation can simply mean looking at the injuries you've had in the past and trying to do targeted exercises to strengthen the affected areas and avoid future problems. And this is suitable for DIY, if you are careful.

My skier's thumb is an example. Skier's thumb involves damage to the ulnar collateral ligament at the base of the thumb. The damage is usually caused when the thumb is pulled away from the hand in a fall. The pole strap is often the mechanical cause of this, as it exerts significant leverage on the joint as you fall.

The post-injury rehabilitation approach to skier's thumb usually involves movement exercises to restore range of motion, combined with progressive resistance exercises to restore strength in the surrounding muscles.

A prehabilitation approach would involve taking a selection of the same sort of exercises and including them in your pre-season training. So, for a previously-damaged thumb you would do some range-of-motion exercises. And you would do things to help build strength — like squeezing a tennis ball or pushing your thumb out against light resistance bands.

Another possible exercise would be to hold a bath towel and twist and squeeze it, as if you were wringing it out. However this exercise shows that you need to be a little careful with prehab routines. Skier's thumb was once more commonly known as gamekeeper's thumb, after the Scottish gamekeepers' practice of killing rabbits by wringing their necks. So, go easy with the towel. For if you wring it too often or too vigorously, you may incur precisely the kind of injury you are trying to prevent.

As a starting point for this kind of prehab, I think it's useful to look at websites specialising in physiotherapy or sports injury. Check out the standard post-injury rehabilitation exercises for your own specific injury or weakness and then work them up carefully into a programme that maintains range of motion and progressively builds local strength.

Section 8
Fitness Equipment

8.1 Nordic Track machines 1

Posted on 24 September 2006

As winter approaches and the days grow shorter it becomes more difficult to train in the open air, and we look for activities we can do indoors. One option is the ski-simulator sold under the brand name Nordic Track.

I bought one in the early 1990s. Though it provides a fairly good simulation of classic-style XC skiing, there are some important differences.

When using your arms, you don't push back on poles. Rather, you pull back on a single continuous cord wound around a tensioned spindle. As you bring back your right hand, your left hand is pulled forward, and vice-versa. This arrangement is fine in terms of muscle workout: triceps and shoulders get particular benefit. But in terms of skiing technique it does tend to make you shorten your arm-extension.

When using your legs, you don't kick down and back. If you did, your feet would simply pop out of the toe-loops that serve as bindings. Rather, you slide your "skis" forward, rolling them over wheels and against a tensioned flywheel. This takes a bit of getting used to; and even when you are used to it you will probably think it's the weakest aspect of the design.

(I tried removing the standard "skis" and replacing them with proper track skis. But they were too noisy and too bumpy. I then thought about attaching proper XC bindings to the standard "skis", but decided against it. If I lost balance — or absent-mindedly tried to jump off to answer the phone — a broken leg would be a certainty.)

So using a Nordic Track can feel very different from skiing, and a potential drawback is that it might spoil your ski technique. More certain drawbacks are that the machine takes a lot of space and is noisy. If you live in a flat it is not a very good option. Even if you live in a large house, the best place for it is probably the garage.

On the plus side, the Nordic Track gives a low impact workout that is relatively ski-specific. Even on low resistance settings your heart rate will quickly rise to effective training levels. You can alter the intensity by raising the height of the front feet or by changing the resistance of the flywheel. The skiing movement is pleasantly rhythmic and XC enthusiasts will probably find themselves closing their eyes and imagining themselves on some favourite ski route.

The machines seem to have come down in price over the years, but still retail at a fairly hefty £399 (including delivery to UK addresses). However from time to time you see them on eBay, often priced about £50 and almost always offered on the basis of "buyer-collects".

8.2 Wobble boards

Posted on 29 October 2006

Of all the different aspects of fitness, balance is one of the hardest to train for, especially if you are a new skier. There are some very good forms of balance-based exercise around, like yoga and Pilates, but they aren't ski-specific and their benefits can therefore take a while to work through. On the other hand, many of the activities that are ski-related — for example ice-skating, rollerskiing and dry-slope skiing — demand that you already have pretty good balance before you can even attempt them. So it can be hard to find a starting point.

But it's not impossible. In this posting we look at a simple but effective piece of balance-promoting equipment, the wobble board.

Wobble-boards are mainly used by physiotherapists and sports injury professionals, and are chiefly employed to help patients recover from injuries to the ankle or lower leg. They are not expensive. I recently bought one from a supplier of sports medical and rehabilitation products for just over £17. It is 36cm (14 inches) in diameter and is made of plastic. It sits on a base of bevelled plastic that is about 11cm (4 inches) in diameter. Imagine a big dinner-plate sitting on half a grapefruit.

Balance benefits — beginners

If you are new to skiing, then it's best to stand on the wobble-board with both feet. Keep your feet about shoulder-width apart and try to adopt the basic "alpine" stance: knees slightly bent, arms a little forward and out to your sides, body-weight equally shared between both feet. Initially you should hold on to a chair for support. You can then get used to the board by rocking it gently backwards and forwards, and then from side to side.

Then let go of the chair, and see if you can stay level. It can be tricky. You will feel yourself pitching about as you lose your balance, regain it, then lose it again. This gets quite close to the feeling of skiing down a descending track on which there are bumps and dips and twists and turns.

When you have gotten the hang of it, the usual progression is simply to stay on the board for longer, trying to keep in balance. However, to make the sessions more challenging, you can do other exercises while on the board — like raising your arms to shoulder-height, then above your head, then lowering them back to your sides. Or you can bend your knees, drop slowly into a crouch for a few moments, and then stand tall.

Balance benefits — experienced skiers

Boards are also used by more experienced skiers. In particular, racers use them when training for classic-technique events. Their main aim is to make sure that when they are skiing they keep their ski bases absolutely flat to the snow (rather than coming up on to their edges, which will slow them down).

To achieve this aim you should stand on your wobble-board on just one foot. (But do practise beforehand on both feet, to get the feel of the board.) Standing one-footed on the centre of the board, first simply try to achieve balance. Then crouch into a more dynamic skiing position, as if you were in the glide phase of diagonal stride. Then do what you have to do to stop wobbling! It may be that you have to push your knee out, to bring it over your toes. Watch yourself in a mirror. And hold on to a chair to begin with. Work equally on both sides.

As a by-product of all these balance exercises, you'll get the bonus of a muscle endurance benefit, mainly in the calves and thighs. (And that's another way of saying that you can get tired very quickly. So take it easy until you are sure of your balance.)

8.3 Nordic Track machines 2

Posted on 22 July 2007

Back in September 2006 we posted a general article about Nordic Track exercisers. Recently an exchange of emails on another XC web forum has brought the machines back into focus. One member of that forum asked: "Does anyone have any advice for use of a Nordic Track ski machine for training and its suitability? eBay is now littered with second-hand Nordic Track machines."

Two other members responded. One said, "Personal experience of Nordic Track machines is not good in terms of technique, or fitness." Another said: "Having tried a Nordic Track a few years ago, it's nothing like the real thing and I can't say it gave me much of a workout or did a great deal for my stamina. Could that be why eBay is so well populated with them?!"

I thought this was a little harsh, especially the last bit. After all, eBay is populated with all sorts of fitness kit, not just ski machines. (A recent survey, reported in *Fitpro Network* magazine in April/May 2007, found that one fifth of all the fitness gadgets bought in Britain each year are used only once — or never at all.) And the fact that something is on eBay may just mean that it is unwanted, rather than unsatisfactory.

Our own September 2006 posting had said that the Nordic Track machine "gives a low impact workout that is relatively ski-specific. Even on low resistance settings your heart rate will quickly rise to effective training levels." In spite of the comments on the other web forum I still believed that statement to be true, but I had to admit I had never been very scientific about the way I used my own machine. I usually just climbed aboard and worked at a reasonable pace for a while. I seldom measured my work-rate.

So in the last week I've tried to rectify that, bench-testing the machine in a range of fitness workouts, each time using a heart-rate monitor to track energy expenditure.

(If you are new to training with a monitor, the first thing to do is establish your Maximum Heart Rate [MHR]. The quick and dirty way is to start with the number 220 and then subtract your age in years. So, if you are aged 40 your MHR will be 180. Once you know your own MHR you train at varying percentages of it - depending on what type of fitness benefit you are trying to achieve in each workout.)

I did five sessions in the course of the week.

Monday: 30 minutes steady-state at about 70-75% MHR.

I started too slowly and took a few minutes to get into the target training zone. However, once in the zone the problem was keeping within it and not drifting higher — it was such a comfortable workout.

Tuesday: medium-length, medium-intensity intervals at about 80% MHR.

A 15 minute warm-up on the machine got me gradually to 70% MHR. Then six 3-minute bursts at just over 80% MHR with one-minute recoveries. Then warm-down on the machine for 10 minutes.

Once again the main problem was keeping within the target zone during the intervals. I often hit 85% MHR and had to ease off.

Wednesday: "recovery workout" at about 65% MHR.

I did 30 minutes at 65% MHR then 5 minutes warm-down. It felt very, very relaxed. I had expected this to be the most difficult session to control, as in the previous two workouts my HR had always edged higher and higher. In fact it was easy and I was only ever about 3 beats off target.

Thursday: short-length, high-intensity intervals at about 90% MHR.

A 15 minute warm-up on the machine gradually got me up to 75% MHR. Then five 1-minute intervals, with 3-minute recovery periods.

This wasn't very successful. I could only reach to the target when I was about 45 seconds into the interval. The problem arose partly because it is difficult to make quick adjustments to the machine. But it was also because a 3-minute recovery is really a bit too long. Normally I would have gone for 1-minute intervals and 1-minute recoveries — and I think that would have worked well. But in the last month I've had a lay-off with a chest infection and I just didn't want to work that hard.

Friday: steady-state workout at race pace (85% MHR).

A 15 minute warm-up got me gradually up to 75% MHR. Then 30 minutes at 85% MHR. Then 15-minute warm-down.

This was hard work, but manageably so.

Conclusions

Although I've had my Nordic Track for many years, I was surprised this week to discover how versatile and effective it is. The versatility allowed me to try different sorts of workout. The effectiveness had two aspects: I could work quite hard, yet it seldom actually felt hard. (In fitness jargon the "rate of perceived exertion" is low.) There are other things I can do to get my HR up to 85% — Nordic walking on hills, for example. But I'm not sure I could sustain them enjoyably for 30 minutes at a time.

The main problem with exercise machines is usually boredom. And until now I've usually found that half an hour on the Nordic Track was enough. This week, though, the machine sessions were actually interesting, largely because I was always focussing on stop-watch and heart-rate monitor, rather than simply plodding along. Nevertheless, I just couldn't stomach the thought of the lengthy endurance sessions that were needed to balance the fairly short periods described above. I really should have done a couple of 2-hour workouts at low intensity on the machine. But as the sun was shining I chose instead to grab my Nordic walking poles and head off to the park. Much nicer!

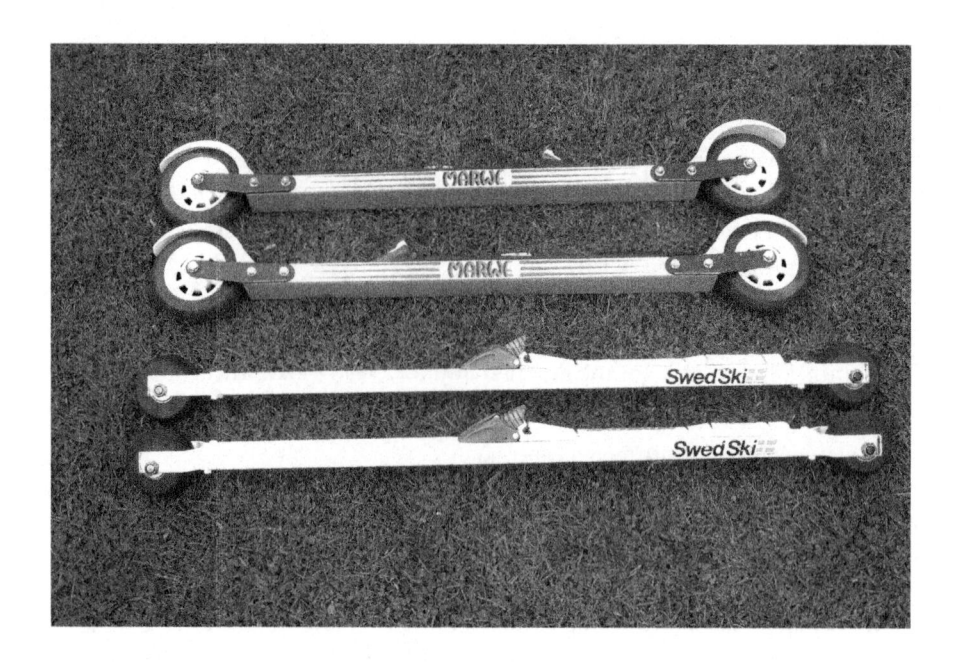

8.4 Rollerski maintenance

Posted on 4 November 2011

Rollerski equipment (like everything else) needs to be maintained. In the last few months I've clocked hundreds of kilometres on my classic rollers and in that time I've had to replace a set of bindings and a pole ferrule, and I've re-greased the bearings on all four wheels. In addition I've generally tried to keep everything in working order and, importantly, in a clean and hygienic state.

It hasn't been rocket science. Generally I've needed the same level of skill and the same kinds of tools I'd use when servicing my bicycle, say, or the lawnmower.

Replacing bindings

"James Bond clipped into his beloved Marwe Six-Tens and smiled into the warm brown eyes of Miss Moneypenny" is a sentence you can confidently expect never to see in print. When it comes to dash and glamour, rollerskiing is irretrievably beyond the pale. It is futile to imagine, although some people do, that in our knee and elbow pads, bike helmets and improbable shorts we will ever impress anyone.

Which helps explain why for years I happily stayed faithful to my ancient Salomon 301 bindings. Once considered cutting-edge, passing time has lent them a sort of antique status, and other skiers now bestow upon them the kind of smile usually reserved for cars with wooden window frames. I liked them fine, and would have cheerfully squeezed another couple of decades out of them, but finally this summer my last pair of compatible boots gave out.

So it was time to replace them — with a pair of SNS Profils, themselves also now outmoded, but I've had them lying around for years and still have two pairs of compatible boots.

Changing the bindings has been the hardest piece of recent maintenance. Although I had taken advice from people who fit a lot of bindings and had been assured I would not need to drill new screw-holes, in fact I did need to do so. However, the new holes would have been extremely close to the old ones, which would have weakened the shafts, so I decided to swap round the front and rear wheels, reversing the direction of travel of the rollers. This gave me more space for drilling.

The paper template that came with the new bindings was accurate and simple to use, but even so I was always aware that it would be very easy to drill the new holes just a little off-centre and thus effectively ruin the rollerskis. Next time I will either invest in a drilling-jig or get a shop to do the job for me.

Changing pole ferrules

I needed to do this after the metal tip on one pole snapped off. Replacing the tip meant changing the entire ferrule, the plastic sleeve on which the metal tip is mounted. It turned out to be an easy job. Luckily the old one had been fixed with hot-melt glue, so it came off quickly and cleanly after I had immersed it in very hot water for a few minutes.

Fitting the new ferrule was also straightforward. I used an electric glue gun to melt the new glue. (I did complicate matters by doing this job out-of-doors on a cold morning. This meant the glue hardened too quickly, and I had to soften it by dipping pole and ferrule again in hot water.) If you don't have a gun it is possible to melt a glue stick by setting it alight, but it is not nearly as safe. Once I had fitted the new ferrule I applied some non-soluble glue around the metal tip, to strengthen its bond to the ferrule.

(If you are thinking of buying a stock of spare ferrules, be aware that they come in various sizes, the different pole manufacturers using different diameters.)

Re-greasing bearings

This was easier than I had feared. For my front wheels (which do not have a ratchet) the process was:

- Remove the wheel and place it in a vice, with the spindle vertical.
- Tap out the spindle using a rubber-headed mallet.
- With the spindle removed, pull or tap away the bearings.
- Gently prise off the washers from each side of the bearings. This exposes the ball-race, which will be covered in old grease.
- Remove the old grease. (I have read that you are not supposed to use solvent, a piece of advice that I might file under Romantic Notions.)
- Apply new grease. I used general-purpose grease, which works well enough but it does make the wheels slower. That's fine for training, but if I was a racer I'd want to use something lighter, like the lithium greases you can buy in cycle shops.
- Reassemble.

The process with the rear wheels was similar, but was complicated slightly by the ratchet mechanism, the thing that allows the wheel to move forward but not back. Mine comprises a group of four springs attached to the spindle, interspaced with four cylindrical rollers. Once dismantled it was a simple-to-understand, if ingenious, contraption. But it was fiddly to handle and if I was not careful enough, which I repeatedly wasn't, then the entire gubbins would spill out and scatter to the dark corners of the workshop floor.

I'm not sure how often you are supposed to re-grease rollerskis. But I should probably do it more often than most people, because after each session, out at Dorney Rowing Lake, I make sure to dip my rollers into the lake.

Cleaning the rollerskis

Immersing mechanical objects in water is seldom a good thing, but I'm provoked into it by Canada Geese. Three statistics will explain this:

1 Geese defecate from 30 to 90 times a day.

2 The average Canada Goose dropping has a dry weight of 1.2gm.

3 A local bird-watcher has recorded seeing as many as 120 of the birds, at one time, on a field near the lake.

I tend to do my rollerskiing first thing in the morning, when it is often abundantly clear that many of the birds have roosted overnight on the tarmac tracks that I am using. The geese have as much right as me to be there, and I love to see them flying overhead, but skiing through their poo is low on my list of favourite things. Which is why the rollers get their dip in the lake-water.

Back at the car I wash them again in clean water, then spray them (and my boots and poles) with disinfectant. The kit partly dries while I do my post-workout stretches, and then everything goes into a large paper refuse sack before being stowed in the boot of the car. (In the paper sack it can continue to dry out, whereas if I used a plastic bag it would not.)

I'm aware that there is an extremely polarised debate about the health risks posed by Canada Geese and I'm trying not to get involved in it.

Some people claim that the birds pose a huge threat to humankind and should be slaughtered wholesale. Other people insist that there are no proven health issues. On one goose-friendly website, I've read that the droppings are merely "recycled grass".

And so, of course, they are. But, like the pieces of recycled Winalot that I also sometimes encounter, I prefer to wash them away.

Section 9

Nordic Walking

9.1 Not just a stroll in the park

Posted on 17 April 2006

A version of this article first appeared in Ski Nordic magazine in 2005.

Nordic walking is enjoying a surge of popularity in Europe and Scandinavia. An estimated 3.5 million people practise it regularly, and the number is growing quickly: sales of walking poles are outstripping sales of ski poles. This success is partly due to some clever marketing by fitness organisations and pole manufacturers — who have taken a broad approach and emphasised that the activity can bring health and fitness benefits to a very wide range of people, almost irrespective of age or physical ability.

A downside of this promotional strategy is that Nordic walking can become perceived as rather a soft exercise, with little obvious appeal to fit people wanting a serious workout. The aim of this article is to counter that view. Let's remember, after all, that Nordic walking started out (in Finland in the 1930s) as a highly focused form of training for elite XC racers who sought to maintain peak fitness during the off-season.

Basically, Nordic walking is walking with poles. The usual formula for determining pole length is to take your height and multiply it by 0.68. When standing at ease and holding the pole upright, your elbow should be at 90 degrees. This means that your correct walking poles will be a lot shorter than your skiing poles, perhaps 25 cm shorter than for classic skiing.

Once suitably equipped, you can simply head off to your local park and start walking. INWA, the International Nordic Walking Association, has set out three broad levels of participation.

Level 1 ("health" level) involves walking at an easy pace with a normal gait. Poling is light, with shoulders relaxed. You keep your hands low as they go forward, and push back only until your hand is level with your hip. It feels like very gentle cross-country skiing — a sort of shortened diagonal stride with a restricted arm action. This level is intended for people who are unused to exercise, and the recommendation is for daily sessions of about 15-30 minutes duration. Although even such low-intensity poling will exercise and tone the upper body, the main benefit is the cardio-vascular workout.

Walking at this level is also useful technical preparation for XC skiing. Novice skiers have many skills to master on their first winter holiday, and their learning curve will be much less daunting if they are already confident with poles before venturing on to snow.

Level 2 is the "fitness" level, and here things become more interesting for the seasoned XC skier. Poling should be firmer, with a pronounced push-back — just like in classic-style skiing — in which the hand releases only after it passes the hip. The walking action should emphasise an initial heel-plant, then an unrolling of the foot from heel to toe before a definite push off from the ball of the foot. Stride should lengthen and walking speed should increase — aim for 3.5 mph or more. You should swagger a little, to increase the body's rotation (as your pelvis rotates in one direction your shoulders rotate in the other). But the shoulders remain relaxed.

If you walk like this for an hour, it is said, you will burn 400-500 kilocalories while exercising 90% of your main muscles. At the time you may not be aware how hard you are working — studies have found that Nordic walking has a low rate of perceived exertion (RPE). But afterwards you will definitely feel the effects. If you can manage three sessions a week at this level you will soon notice a marked improvement in fitness (and in appearance, if my own experience is typical: in six months I lost over a stone).

To increase the intensity of your Nordic walking you can introduce hill work or — if you live by the sea — walk on soft sand. Or you can try *fartlek*, which is an irregular mix of "work" and "active recovery". A typical *fartlek* session would combine bursts of slow and fast walking, with the fast bursts making up the work phases, But you can, if you prefer, concentrate the work into the slow phases, simply by poling very strongly during them.

Level 3 is the "sport" level. Here the idea is to combine brisk Nordic walking and high-intensity exercises involving running, leaping and bounding. Some of the routines are very strenuous and put heavy strain on joints and muscles, so do proceed with caution.

For example, start with a few minutes of brisk Nordic walking then introduce short bursts of running. To begin with you should carry your poles while running, and only start to pole when you have found an easy running rhythm.

Next, introduce short bursts of skipping, as a child would skip. Then try some bounding, which is slow running with a long, springy gait. Again, do these exercises first without poles, and only introduce poling action when you have found a rhythm.

Next you can try some two-footed bunny hops, and when you have found a rhythm you can introduce a little double-poling to help yourself along.

From bunny hops you can make the transition to skate-bounding, which involves springing obliquely forward from one foot to the other.

Now and again you can come to a stop, hold your poles a little wider than hip width for support, and jump up and down on the spot, as if you were skipping with a rope. Once you are used to it, push down on your poles to make yourself jump higher.

You can treat such routines as unstructured *fartlek*, making up the "programme" as you go, and — if you feel like it — increasing the intensity by running faster or leaping higher. Alternatively you can put together fixed sessions of circuit training. For example, on a short triangular course, with sides about 20 metres long, try the following:

- walk round the triangle five times, alternating fast and slow sides.
- do one side slow, one side skipping, one side slow, followed by 20 static jumps. Repeat five times.
- do one side slow, one side bunny-hops assisted by double-poling, one side slow, followed by 20 static jumps. Repeat five times.
- finish by running round 3 times, then walk a few times to warm down.

This is just an example, not a prescription. You can have a lot of fun developing your own circuits and tailoring them to meet your personal fitness goals.

9.2 Hill work with poles

Posted on 23 June 2006

Hill work with poles has been used for decades by XC racers and is universally accepted as an essential element of any programme of dryland training for serious skiers. However it has tended to be spurned by recreational skiers, who see it as just too hard for them.

Nordic walking's increasing popularity may change that view. The new sport is attracting a wide range of people, not all of whom are — by any means — super-fit. Yet in parks and open spaces throughout Britain they regularly and without complaint include hill work in their training.

When faced with an uphill slope, standard Nordic walking technique calls for you to lean into the hill a little, to pole firmly, and to lengthen your stride. You are still walking, in the sense that you always have at least one foot on the ground at all times. Because you have lengthened your stride, the hamstring and calf muscles are worked and developed. And because you are poling firmly, the muscles of your arms, shoulders and back are also worked. Finally, because your heart rate will rise to quite a high level (you do need to be careful, and a heart rate monitor is useful) stamina is improved. Provided that you choose a hill with a good, even surface the risk of injury to muscles or joints is low.

If you simply want to improve your overall fitness then including one or two weekly hill sessions like this can be of great benefit. However if you want to develop your classic skiing technique you can shorten your stride, quicken your tempo, and jog up the hill. If you put a spring in your step and concentrate on transferring your body weight from one foot to the other — rocking a little from side to side with each stride — you will simulate the action of flattening your skis down on to the snow to make your wax grip. But even though you may be aiming primarily for a technical benefit — an improvement in skiing skills — the fitness benefit is also very clear, and both stamina and muscle endurance are promoted.

If now, to consider a third variant, you climb the hill by taking longer, more explosive strides and pushing harder with your poles, you move into "ski bounding". You can still use Nordic walking poles for this, though athletic skiers would probably prefer longer poles, perhaps 10cm shorter than their usual classic skiing ones. The benefits are in respect of stamina, muscle endurance and muscle strength. This variant is very strenuous and the risk of muscle strain or joint injury is commensurably high.

You have yet another option — moose hoofs. This term is a translation of the Norwegian word *elghufs*, which is used to suggest the shuffling gait of a moose (or elk). In this variant you keep your stride length fairly short and keep your speed up. The stride is somewhere between walking and running — at times both feet are off the ground, but only very briefly. And you do not lift your feet very high off the ground at any time. The idea is to reduce the muscle strength component and maximise the stamina benefit.

Whichever variant you choose, you need to choose your hill with care. The surface should be as even as possible, and free from potholes and tussocks. And of course the steepness of the hill should be appropriate to your current level of fitness. My own Nordic walking groups use a slope in a public park. It is so gentle that most park users probably don't notice it at all, but it gives us a good enough workout. We take about 50 double-strides to get from bottom to top. We usually start with five up-and-down repetitions and then build up gradually to ten. Usually we employ the standard Nordic walking technique, but with a fit group I will do some moose hoofs.

To consider the other extreme: the current training programme of the Norwegian men's XC team includes moose hoofs in 5 x 5-minutes intervals at a perceived intensity level of 4-5 (hard) with short recovery times.

My Nordic walkers have the Norwegian programme as a goal, of course, but it is for the long term…

9.3 Nordic walking (advanced)

Posted on 6 August 2006

This posting is aimed at people who have already done at least a couple of months of regular Nordic walking at a moderate level, who have coped well with the physical demands, and who now want to increase the intensity. At this time of year, as autumn approaches, many cross-country skiers will be trying to step up their training — and many others will be thinking of making a start! It is hoped that the following can give them some ideas.

The general approach is to borrow training methods from endurance running and adapt them to the requirements and fitness levels of enthusiastic walkers. The specific examples given below are based on work I have been doing with groups in our local park, and they are intended as illustrations rather than prescriptions. A different group using a different park will call for a different schedule.

Generally speaking we try to maintain good technique. The group members all know what to aim for: abdominals engaged, shoulders soft, good pushback of poles. But we are quite prepared occasionally to sacrifice technique for speed in the interest of a good workout, especially on our 5km route, when the improvement of personal best times is a strong motivator.

Our primary aim is to improve stamina, but some of the routines also develop muscle strength and endurance.

All sessions are preceded by appropriate mobilisation exercises and followed by stretching. We meet once a week, and our eight-week programme is a mix of the following elements:

Long, modertate distance. Our park is a venue for Cancer Research's "Race for Life" series, and a 5-kilometre course has been accurately measured and clearly marked. We walk round it at a sustained moderate pace — it feels strenuous and we sweat, but the pace is easy enough to allow some conversation — and we aim to complete the course in less than 50 minutes. This calls for a respectable average speed of at least 6kph (3.75 mph).

Our 5km sessions are taken at sustained intensity. In all our other sessions we stop from time to time to rest and drink, and we always include a lengthy period of slow walking, to allow time for chatting and for warm-down.

Long, slow distance. The park is adjacent to good walking routes on footpaths and bridleways in the parks surrounding the town of Eton and along the Jubilee River, which is a flood relief scheme for the Thames. We have a choice of training routes, each involving about 1.25 hours walking at easy conversational speed.

Short-distance intervals. In a corner of the park there is a square area of level grass with sides approximately 150 metres long. With beginners groups I often use this area for simple intervals, in which we walk one side slowly then one side fast: the work and active recovery phases are of equal distance. But with an advanced group we will do "pyramid" training, in the following sequence and without pausing:

- walk slowly round all four sides to warm up.
- do one side fast, one side slow, one side fast, one side slow.
- do two sides fast and one side slow.
- do three sides fast and one side slow.
- do four sides fast.

Ideally, having climbed up the pyramid of intensity in gradual stages, we should come back down in the same measured way. But as the above sequence will already have involved almost 3km of walking and will have taken about 30 minutes, we usually content ourselves with proceeding to a 30-minute easy-paced walk round the main park perimeter, which we treat as a warm-down.

Long-distance intervals. At the top of our park there is an extensive flat area, about 750 metres in length. As it takes us about seven minutes to walk one length, a session of four lengths is enough to give a satisfactory basic workout.

The most straightforward way to handle this area is simply to alternate easy and hard lengths — to walk slowly in one direction and then come quickly back.

With a very fit group we do a total of six lengths in a pattern of "ladder intervals", in which the speed of each fast length is increased.

Hills. Our park has a short, gentle slope on which we do simple intervals — working hard uphill and recovering on the way back down. Normally we do ten repetitions.

There is also a much longer slope, perhaps 200 metres long, but still very gentle. We currently include this in our 5km circuit, going up and down it twice in the course of one circuit. We plan also to use it for a form of pyramid training. We will start at the bottom and walk up for 100 metres. Then we will return to the bottom and walk up for 110 metres — and so on, increasing the uphill stage by 10 metres each time.

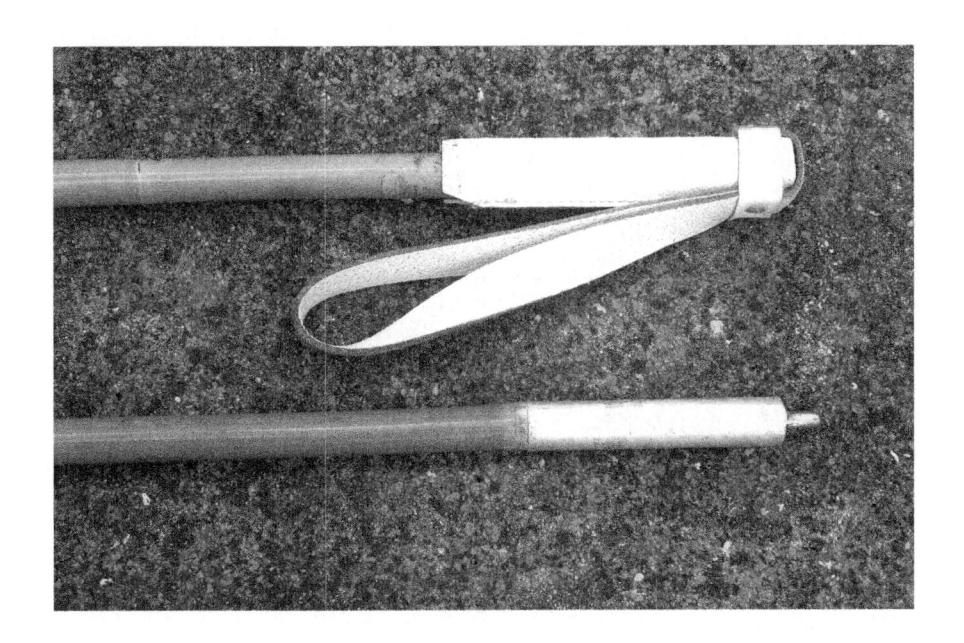

9.4 Making your own poles

Posted on 12 August 2007

Nordic walking enthusiasts like to tell us that their sport can be traced back to the time when top Scandinavian XC racers, wanting to maintain peak fitness year-round, started to use their ski poles during summer "dryland" training sessions. However for many of these enthusiasts this nostalgia for the old ways is limited; and soon they go on to tell us that XC poles are thoroughly unsuitable for Nordic walking (NW). What we need instead, they say, are specially designed NW poles. Anything else will be too heavy, or will have poor shock-absorption or some other vital ergonomic deficiency.

Well, I've never been sure about that. So a couple of winters ago I brought home from Norway some old bamboo XC poles, with the intention of modifying them for NW. And — these things take time — I have finally gotten round to finishing the job. The conclusion is that they work well enough for me.

I bought the poles in a ski hire shop near Lillehammer. The shop-keeper didn't know how much to charge but we settled on 100 kroner per pair, a bit less than £10 Sterling at the going rate of exchange. (They are therefore possibly the cheapest things you can buy in Norway.)

As NW poles are shorter than XC ones, I asked if there were any children's sizes, but there were not. The only sizes available were 150cm or longer, and so I would need to cut them down to my usual 120cm.

What the job involved

The poles are of the sort that was used widely in Scandinavia until maybe 20 years ago. The shaft is made from varnished bamboo, with a diameter of about 16mm. At the top is a white leather handle with a loop of leather. The leather pieces are fixed to the shaft with a hefty rivet.

I don't have tools for riveting, so I didn't want to disturb this top end, just in case I couldn't fit it back together again.

The bottom end looked easier to work with. It has an aluminium ferrule, a sort of sheath about 90mm long. It protects the bottom of the pole, and provides an attachment for the basket and for the spike that is the pole's point of contact with the ground. I decided to shorten this bottom end.

I wanted to keep the ferrules, but I didn't need the baskets, which came off easily (just remove a split pin) and went into my box of ski spares. Removing the ferrules was tricky. One of them slid off after a lot of coaxing. The other seemed to have been fixed with glue. Hoping it was hot-melt glue I tried to soften it in boiling water, but that didn't work. So I had to saw it off then clamp it in a vice and drill it out.

Shortening the shafts to NW length was a two minute job with a sharp saw.

There were then two things to do before refitting the ferrules.

One was to take a file to the outside of the bottom of the poles, to reduce their diameter a little so that they would fit snugly into the ferrules.

The other was to glue a length of dowelling inside the hollow centre of each bamboo shaft. These would provide the bases into which the spikes would be screwed.

Then I refitted the ferrules and glued them in place.

Finally I screwed in the spikes. But (now that the baskets were no longer there to act as fenders) they seemed dangerously long and sharp, so I shortened and blunted them with an angle-grinder. (A hacksaw and file would have done the job just as well, but much more slowly.)

Overall, the project was enjoyable enough, but it was fiddly and it needed more tools (and more time) than I had expected. An alternative and quicker method would be to cut off and discard the original ferrules and baskets and simply attach new walking stick ferrules. You can get them from walking stick specialists. If most of your NW is on hard surfaces you might choose a rubber ferrule. If you walk mostly on grass you might instead choose an "Alpine" ferrule, which has a metal spike.

How the poles perform

Weight-wise, they are not much heavier than specialised NW poles. On our kitchen scales they are about 190gm per pole, just a little more than my Exel Trainers, which are about 170gm.

Performance-wise, they seem fine. The straps don't allow quite as good a push-back as the Exel straps, and they are not quite as comfortable, but the difference is small. The overall handling is good — which is to say, once I have walked with them for a few minutes I more or less forget about them and concentrate on my workout. Shock-absorption seems okay.

So, if you are up for a bit of DIY and you fancy the thought of an inexpensive and environmentally sound piece of fitness kit, then save some room in your ski bag next time you travel to the snow, and get ready to do some haggling in the ski shop.

9.5 Nordic walking and biomechanics

Posted on 4 November 2009

A few weeks ago I attended a course for personal trainers on the subject of "Advanced Functional Training". Its focus was on gym work, but it has carried across to Nordic walking and has suggested ways in which NW workouts can be made more challenging.

The course had two broad themes. The first was chain-reaction biomechanics, which is based on the premise that when you move any one part of your body, many other parts will be affected as a result. Sports coaches use their knowledge of this to improve their students' performance. In boxing, if you want someone to throw a hard punch then you should make them push strongly off their rear foot. In skiing, if a student is struggling to turn their skis down a piste then you may need to change how they hold their shoulders.

If you take a biomechanical approach to Nordic walking, and deliberately vary the ways in which you move your arms and legs, then you can come up with different workouts. You can combine cardio-vascular and strength elements — and achieve a lot of variety in the strength elements.

With NW, as with any activity, you can vary movements through three planes of motion: front to back (known as sagittal), side to side (known, perversely, as frontal) and rotational (known as transverse).

Sagittal plane

When doing NW I usually keep my arm bent at the elbow as I reach forward to plant the pole. I find it a natural movement, perhaps because it seems like the poling movement in classic-style cross-country skiing. The relatively short forward reach also allows me enough time — when it comes to the push-back phase of the poling action — to extend my arm well behind my hip. This again seems like the movement in skiing and it gives me the same kind of triceps workout.

But if I want to do some biomechanical tweaking, then I can keep my arm almost straight throughout the poling movement. This makes my arm into a longer lever. One result is a greater loading on my lower back and abdominal muscles. So, by straightening my arms, I can achieve a pretty good workout for my core muscles.

Another example of sagittal plane tweaking is best done on a hill. Here, I start by jogging (with poles) up the hill using a short stride. In cardio-vascular terms this is moderately hard. But in terms of strength it's easy — the jogging is light on the leg muscles and the poling action is light on the arms. But then I increase my stride length and my speed, so that I am running up the hill in a bounding kind of gait. Okay, I immediately notice a surge in cardio-vascular intensity, but I also feel lots of muscles being worked harder — upper and lower legs as well as arms and shoulders.

Frontal plane

When doing NW I prefer to keep my arms a little distance away from my body as I swing them backwards and forwards. My elbows will be about six inches out from my ribs. This seems a natural, unforced position. But if I now alter the biomechanics by forcing my arms into positions that are less natural, then I can once again change the workout.

If, to begin with, I bring my arms really close in to my body then I'll feel that I am working my triceps very much harder during the push-back.

But if I then extend my arms away from my body (think crucifixion) before pushing on the poles, then I'll feel a much greater loading on my chest and my back.

Transverse plane

When doing NW I prefer to plant my poles just a little obliquely to the line of travel. The idea is to get the shoulders to rotate in one direction while the pelvis rotates in another. The repeated gentle twisting of the spine is good for posture and general strength.

However, if I'm in the mood for a bit of biomechanical tweaking, then I'll try to accentuate the spinal rotation. If I slow my speed right down, and push firmly and obliquely back on the poles, then I'll feel a very intense workout in my oblique (abdominal) muscles and my lower back. And I can increase the intensity further if I walk like a catwalk-model — my feet in a straight line — so as to drive the rotation of my pelvis. And if I over-exaggerate the catwalk-model aspect, by actually crossing my feet in front of each other, then I'll feel the loading on my inner and outer thigh muscles as well.

By now of course we are well into Ministry of Silly Walks territory and the obvious question that poses itself is: "Why bother?"

Well, that's where the second theme of the course I attended comes in: training for function.

Some of the ideas behind training for function can be illustrated by the example of sports coaching. Sportspeople don't want just to be fit or just to have strong muscles. They want to become better at performing a function — a sporting activity. And that function involves a lot of body movements that can be performed more effectively by people who are fit and strong.

Their coaches will prepare them better by prescribing training routines that mimic the body movements required by their sporting activity. Importantly, the routines should ideally cover all the possible movements required in the sport, including the weird, out-of-position moves that will injure you if you have not prepared for them. So, a tennis player will not only practise ground strokes and volleys, but will also prepare for the occasional running-backwards overhand smash.

Which brings us back to Nordic walking. One of the reasons I do NW is to keep in shape for cross-country skiing. The basic movements are similar, and even if I were to do only basic NW then I would prepare my muscles and joints for most of the movements I'll do on skis. But I wouldn't prepare myself for all of them. I wouldn't prepare for the thigh pulls that come from skis breaking through crusty snow; or the shoulder twinges that come from the occasional out-of-balance pole plant; or the back twinges that come from touring with a rucksack; or the myriad muscular consequences of face-planting...

Ordinary Nordic walking won't help me avoid those kinds of injuries. But maybe my silly walks will — by strengthening my muscles and joints and by training them to cope better with the sudden, unusual and unexpected movements that the winter will bring.

I'll know soon enough — the snow is on its way!

Section 10
Bookshelf

10.1 The Complete Guide to Marathon Walking (By Dave McGovern)

Posted on 12 May 2007

The Complete Guide to Marathon Walking, By Dave McGovern

World Class Publications. Second edition 2005

ISBN 0-9662176-2-4

Dave McGovern is a former member of the US National Racewalk Team. During a long career in competitive walking he was National Champion at all distances from 10 to 40 kilometres. He also won the racewalking divisions in several road marathons. He has been a racewalking coach since 1986 and has written two other books about competitive walking.

His book on marathon walking has 212 pages and 26 chapters, plus a little afterword called "Chapter 26.2". It is organised into three sections.

Section 1 (Background) includes a short history of marathon walking as well as some general scene-setting about endurance walking.

Section 2 (Training) contains 12 chapters, only two of which are specific to walking. One of the latter covers race-walking technique. It should be of interest to Nordic walkers, especially as by implication it questions the suitability of their own stride pattern for fast-paced walking.

The other gives 18-week training schedules for marathon walkers at three different standards: beginner, intermediate and advanced.

The other 10 chapters in this section are relevant to people training for any endurance event: walking, running, cross-country skiing or whatever. There is a useful and accessible summary of marathon physiology. It leads into a review of different training methods — long slow distance; threshold (intervals and steady-state); economy repeats and recovery workouts. There are then chapters on overtraining and on coping with injuries, and a short guide to maintaining a training diary.

Section 3 (*The race*) has eight helpful chapters on how to manage the race itself: what to wear, what to eat, what to expect, how to recover afterwards.

This is a really good book. Dave McGovern handles the technical stuff well, when he needs to, but generally he carries the reader along with an easy and very witty style. Although it is written for walkers, the book should be of interest to anyone wanting to train for any kind of endurance event.

I think Nordic walkers will find lots of ideas to help them make their workouts more focussed, more effective and more varied. And anyone training for a cross-country ski marathon will also benefit — from the general advice and from the very motivating style. I had never wanted to walk a marathon before reading this book, but I do now, and I can see how I might use a walking race as a stepping-stone towards a skiing event in the winter.

10.2 Long Distance, a Year of Living Strenuously (By Bill McKibben)

Posted on 23 September 2007

Long Distance, a Year of Living Strenuously, By Bill McKibben

Simon & Schuster, New York, 2000.

ISBN (hardback) 0-684-85597-6 (paperback) 0-452-28270-5)

At the age of 37 Bill McKibben, a prominent US writer and environmental campaigner, was thinking that his life had become too sedentary and bookish. Although he was a keen recreational cross-country skier, he felt that he had never pushed his physical limits, never really tested his body. Out of his unease with that situation came the decision to devote a year of his life to training at (roughly) the same volume and intensity as an Olympic endurance athlete would do. After that year he would spend a winter ski racing.

The book is the story of that time. It starts with his meeting on 1 January 1998 with Rob Sleamaker, author of the influential book *Serious Training for Endurance Athletes*, who agreed to coach him. It concludes with his participation in the Norwegian Birkebeiner race fifteen months later.

In telling the story McKibben covers a lot of ground, mentally as well as physically, and the book serves as a good introduction to cross-country ski racing and to cross-country skiing in general.

He says a lot about endurance training. Sleamaker prescribed a tough programme of about 600 hours training over the 12 months. To begin with, most of it was low-intensity, long-duration work, designed to lay down a good aerobic base. McKibben would grow accustomed to long slow distance runs, up to three hours' duration by the summer. But from the outset he also worked on strength and speed. In describing his workouts he writes about training schedules and periodisation, about exercise physiology and nutrition, and about fitness testing (VO2 max and lactate threshold).

By the September he was training 18 hours a week. But no matter how hard he trains, his outlook remains much more the outlook of an intellectual than an athlete. He has an abiding interest in how much (or how little) the physical training is changing his character, his spirit. He sees similarities between endurance training and meditation. He is curious about the reasons, personal and social, why endurance athletes devote huge hours to training. And, being just as curious as to why ordinary people work out on exercise machinery in gyms, he digresses to consider the growth of the fitness industry.

He writes about the recent history of cross-country skiing in the USA. There was huge growth in the 1970s, a decade that saw Bill Koch win a silver medal at the 1976 Winter Olympic Games in Innsbruck. And the 1980s too were good for US racing: Koch won the World Cup one year and USA had four or five finishing in the top twenty at all the races. But then it all fell away. Race performances worsened and the overall number of American XC skiers declined.

And, of course, he writes about his own races. Almost from the outset, Sleamaker encouraged McKibben to compete, and in the first months of training he took part in a race in New England, an event in the Canadian Keskinada festival, and in the World Masters Championships at Lake Placid. Six months into the year he flew to Australia and raced in the Paddy Pallin Classic, a 25km event near Mount Kosciusko.

And he did, finally, have his winter of racing. But it was truncated by the terminal illness of his father. And the suffering and passing of his father comes rather to dominate the end of the story. Some readers will think this enriches the book. Others will feel that it derails it, and that a more focussed volume would in the end have served as a better monument to his father's memory. Nevertheless, the book is a good one, and it deserves a place on the shelf of anyone who has an interest in cross-country skiing.

10.3 Momentum: Chasing the Olympic Dream (By Pete Vordenberg)

Posted on 10 October 2007

Momentum: Chasing the Olympic Dream, By Pete Vordenberg

Out Your Backdoor Press, Williamston MI, 2002

ISBN 1-892590-56-5

This is a brilliant book. When I bought it I read it from cover to cover three times in a row, even though there were lots of other things I should have been doing.

It is the story of a young American's attempt to become an Olympic cross-country ski champion, of how his early dream developed into a firm commitment, and of how he lived and worked when pursuing it.

Sports biography is hard to write, for the lives of athletes — endurance athletes in particular — are not in the main exciting. As Vordenberg himself says, for most of the year the life of a ski racer can be described as "eat, sleep, train . . . eat, sleep, train . . . eat, sleep, train".

He makes his own biography interesting by opting for an episodic structure, rather than a strict chronology. The book opens in 1993, with an account of a summer-long training stint in Southern Washington State.

Vordenberg was then 21 years old, yet he had been training hard for years. He had kept a workout diary since the age of 12, and had nursed Olympic ambitions since his mid-teens. As the book proceeds he flashes back to adolescence in Boulder, Colorado, and to his years as a scholarship student at Northern Michigan University, all the time training hard and finally making the US team for the 1992 Olympics in Albertville. Then he takes the story forward through the 1994 Games in Lillehammer.

The book succeeds on many levels. Athletic skiers will like the technical content. If you want to know about periodised training schedules, then you'll enjoy the excerpts from his diaries from summer and winter 1997 when he was logging 30 hours of hard physical preparation a week; and you'll find many other useful snippets throughout the book. If you want to improve your technique you'll mull over the descriptions of power and glide, "explosion and calm".

But the technical stuff is interwoven nicely with amusing, interesting and sometimes moving accounts of incidents and people, and you can enjoy the book even if you know very little about skiing (though you'll pick up a lot of knowledge in the reading of it).

There is a good human story in the writer's successes and failures in races, and there are some gripping accounts of major events. There's another good story in the way he quietly copes with the chronic lack of funding: by doing manual work in a national park, and by getting into a college for a year in Mora, Sweden, where skiing was a major curriculum subject. "Being an elite cross-country ski racer in America can be compared to going through medical school while being homeless", he says, highlighting the clash between high performance expectations and inadequate support systems.

There is a good collection of well-chosen and well-told anecdotes — about adolescent romance, student high-jinks, alarming nutrition (at a notable post-exercise dinner each member of the university ski team puts away five platefuls of pasty and mashed potatoes). There are surreal episodes: a training run with a Bigfoot hunter in south Washington, a downtime period with flamboyant ex-pat dropouts on a beach in Mexico.

And there is a love story, which comes near the end of the book at an otherwise low point in the adventure, a point at which you will be thinking, this guy could do with a bit of happiness.

Vordenberg writes mainly in an easy, freewheeling style that has been compared with that of Jack Kerouac. Some sections of the book justify that comparison, but others don't. For example:

"How many chances do you get to really do something? One? None? You might get ten but you don't know that. How many chances to you get to be great? Maybe one. So there had better be some urgency, some serious one-shot intensity, because this is it."

Passages like that help explain why Pete Vordenberg got into coaching when his own racing career came to an end. He is now Head Coach of the U.S. Cross Country Ski Team.

Footnote: Pete Vordenberg resigned from the U.S. Cross Country Ski Team in 2012, to spend more time with his growing family.

10.4 The First Crossing of Greenland (By Fridtjof Nansen)

Posted on 5 November 2007

The First Crossing of Greenland, by Fridtjof Nansen

Birlinn, Edinburgh. 2002   ISBN 1-84158-216-6

This is an abridged version of Nansen's classic *På Ski Over Grønland*, which was originally published in Norwegian in 1890 and was then soon translated into several other languages. It tells the story of how in 1888 the explorer, with a team of five, made the first complete traverse of Greenland.

The team's project was an audacious one. They would start from the uninhabited east coast and make for the inhabited west. Nansen's typically uncompromising rationale for doing the journey in that direction was that it would remove the temptation to turn back if they encountered problems. There would be no choice but to go forward.

Of central importance to Nansen was that the party should travel on skis, and in selecting his men he insisted that they were experienced skiers. Chapter two of the book is devoted to a history and description of skiing, "since so little is known about the sport outside the few countries where it is practised as such". It is a factual account, with information about ski construction and skiing technique. But it also contains some very enthusiastic promotion of the sport, as both a recreational and a competitive activity. For example:

"I know no form of sport which so evenly develops the muscles, which renders the body so strong and elastic, which teaches so well the qualities of dexterity and resource, which in an equal degree calls for decision and resolution, and which gives the same vigour and exhilaration to mind and body alike."

The eventual success of the expedition not only brought Nansen enormous publicity and honour but also contributed to a massive upsurge of interest in skiing throughout Europe and North America.

However, before the team members could show the effectiveness of their skis, they first had to make it to the east coast of Greenland, and this in itself was a major adventure that takes up almost half of the book. Setting out from Oslo at the beginning of May, they took one steamer from Oslo to Leith, then another via the Faroes to Iceland. Here they joined a sealing ship that would "do its best to put us ashore on the east coast of Greenland". In the event it was 17 July before they disembarked from the sealer and set off in their small boats.

They had just ten miles of ice-floe to negotiate before landfall. But they were soon caught up in a strong current that carried them southwards and away from land, and it took them twelve days of very hazardous drifting before they did reach land, very much further south than they had intended. They had to fight back northwards in their boats, keeping very close to the coast, and it was mid-August before they reached a point at which they could begin their traverse of the Inland Ice.

The traverse itself was hardly a pleasant journey. First came the ascent on to the ice, negotiating treacherous snow-covered crevasses. ("As a matter of fact, we fell through rarely, and then only to our armpits".) During this period it poured continuously with rain. More bad weather befell them as they gained height, and at one point they were unable to leave camp for three days. Finally they reached more gently sloping ground, and calmer weather, and climbed to an eventual height of just under 8,000 feet. "All this time", wrote Nansen, "our life was simply inordinately monotonous, with not a trace of any important occurrence."

By now it was early September and the lateness of the season brought fresh snow, which impeded their progress and drifted at night through the many openings of their tent. And it grew very cold: one night their thermometer recorded minus 40 degrees Centigrade.

With much effort and much danger they finally made it, on 26 September and after about six weeks on the Inland Ice, to the shores of the west coast.

It took more adventure, including the construction of a makeshift boat from their sledges and tarpaulins, before they reached the safety of the Danish settlement at Godthaab. Here they found they had missed the last steamer of the year, and would need to spend the winter at the settlement.

When Nansen and the team finally made it back to Norway on 30 May in the following year they were welcomed as heroes. A flotilla of sailing boats met them in Christiania (Oslo) Fjord, a crowd of 60,000 people was waiting by the pier, and 50,000 followed them through the streets to their hotel.

This account of their adventure is a nicely solid volume of about 300 pages, enlivened by some original photographs and drawings. It's a good book to curl up with on a dark winter's evening.

10.5 Worldloppet thirtieth anniversary

Posted on 30 November 2007

Worldloppet, the international federation of cross-country ski marathon races, will next year celebrate 30 years of existence, and to mark the anniversary it has just published a book. Titled *Worldloppet — 30 years of skiing around the world*, the book has been edited mainly by Epp Paal, who manages the office of Tartu Maraton, Estonia's Worldloppet race. Epp has obviously put heart and soul into the project and she has produced a very attractive hardback volume. In format it is a little bigger than A4 and it has 167 pages, many of them illustrated in full colour.

The famous Norwegian racer Bjørn Daehlie sets the scene in a brief foreword. He writes: "The Worldloppet Ski Federation sets up a new way of life for thousands of popular cross country skiers, travelling around the world, meeting new people, experiencing foreign traditions, skiing the most important and beautiful XC ski races in the world." And "thousands" is no exaggeration. Each year around 90,000 skiers participate in at least one of the fourteen Worldloppet races, and the number of Worldloppet Masters (people who have completed ten or more races) has now reached almost 2,500.

The book itself opens with "A short history of skiing", an interesting overview contributed by Paddy Field. Later, at the end of the book, he adds a further historical chapter on the introduction (or, as he insists, the re-introduction) of the skating technique by Pauli Siitonen and Bill Koch in the 1970s.

A chapter by Tom Kelly tells the story of the setting up of the Worldloppet Federation in 1978. For many years Kelly was the PR director for Tony Wise, an American entrepreneur who founded the Telemark Ski Lodge in Wisconsin in the late 1940s. Initially the lodge catered only for downhill skiers, but in winter 1972-73 Wise opened a network of cross-country trails and also inaugurated the XC race that would become the American Birkebeiner. Once that was established he then worked hard for several years to persuade eight other marathon race organisers to join together in the cooperative association that was initially called the World Loppet League. The chapter gives an informative and inspiring account.

There is then a chapter on more recent organisational developments. Unless you're a devotee you'll want to skim most of this. But if you are a devotee you will enjoy reading of the expansion from nine to fourteen main races, the growth in the number of races with subsidiary events, and the increasingly close tie-up with FIS (the International Ski Federation).

Then there is a list of all 2461 Worldloppet Masters. Twenty-four of the names are from Great Britain.

Next come fourteen chapters that describe in detail all the Worldloppet races.

These chapters together form by far the largest section of the book. For each race you can see its date of inauguration, its present place in the calendar (e.g. second Sunday of March), the main race distance and whether it is classic or freestyle, details of any short races, the highest number of participants, any years in which the main event was cancelled through bad conditions, and the race organiser's web address. There is also a complete list of the winners. Each chapter also contains a brief history of the event and a description of the area.

In these chapters you can also pick up some quite esoteric information. You can learn that an Estonian prime minister has participated in the Tartu Maraton and that a Eurovision song contest winner has done the Finlandia — as has Tomohito, prince of Japan. And you can learn that the motto of Italy's representative race is *The Marcialonga, a crusade of men rebelling against the slow death of modern life.*

Mostly, though, these chapters contain pictures. Lots of pictures. Some are quaint and historic, like the Tartu racers of 1984 warming tarry wax into their skis over a log bonfire. Some are touching, like the children in the American Birkebeiner kids' event, skating unsteadily away from the start-line. Some are wholly inexplicable, like the pair of fully-grown elephants outside the Tartu Maraton office. But most are just straightforwardly inspiring. If you've never done the Engadin, to take just one example, the iconic shot of the course wending across the ice-bound lake near Silvaplana will make you want to do it. And if you have already done it, the picture will make you want to do it again.

The Worldloppet Federation is taking a very generous attitude towards pricing, and is selling the book, through its website, for just ten euros. Even more generously, the federation has made it available online, free of charge. If you go to *www.worldloppet.com/anniversary_book.php* you will see a thumbnail of every page. And if you click on any thumbnail you then get a full-size pdf of that page.

Footnote: the number of Worldloppet races has now risen to 20.

10.6 A Medal of Honor (By John Morton)

Posted on 23 November 2008

A Medal of Honor, by John Morton

(Second edition)   Discover History LLC, 29 Dec 2005

ISBN-10: 19294043   ISBN-13: 978-1929401048

Very few novels about cross-country skiing have been written in English, so John Morton's story of elite biathlon racing deserves attention on grounds of rarity alone. But, as a bonus, it's also a good read.

A Medal of Honor tells the story of Matt Johnson, a young biathlete from Vermont whose sporting ability brings him to the attention of the US Biathlon Team. He is invited to participate in the National Championships at Lake Placid. He does well, and is therefore asked to attend a US Biathlon Team summer camp a few months later. At this camp the Team members are subjected to "the most comprehensive physiological testing ever administered to American biathletes".

Matt Johnson again does well and gains selection to the team. And, as is proper in a good sporting tale, that selection catapults him into a hectic programme of travel to exotic locations: Alaska, Norway and the Alps. Training and racing become the overwhelming focus of the young man's life. But they are not the only focus, for there is also family conflict; there is romance; and there is personal rivalry within the team. And — especially towards the end of the tale, by which time Johnson is representing his country in a fictional Winter Olympic Games in the Italian Dolomites — there is the seductive distraction of corporate sponsorship and there is the ever-present temptation to use illicit methods to enhance performance.

The tale is well constructed and well told. This was John Morton's first novel, but it doesn't have the uncertain feel of a first novel. Perhaps this is because Morton had served his apprenticeship as a writer some years before embarking upon *A Medal of Honor*. His earlier book, called *Don't Look Back* (1990) was a non-fiction guide to cross-country skiing and racing. It had drawn heavily on Morton's own skiing career, a distinguished career which he summarises thus: "I've had the amazing good fortune to have participated in seven Winter Olympic Games as an athlete, a coach, the U.S. Biathlon Team Leader, or most recently at Salt Lake, as Chief of Course for the Biathlon events."

A Medal of Honor also draws richly upon that background. And into his tale Morton weaves details of training schedules, information about physiological testing, and even guidance on how to zero a biathlon rifle in windy conditions. In the main this factual material fits nicely into the narrative and makes the story more credible and more interesting.

Now and again — it has to be said — the storyline errs somewhat on the side of hard-to-credit, but most skiers will forgive Morton for that and will simply enjoy the yarn.

Perhaps less easy to forgive, and certainly quite difficult to understand, are the loose ends that remain at the end of the tale. Mainly these concern the hero's family life which, as described at length in the early chapters, has a dark and mysterious side. His father had died just before the story opens, in a road accident that suggested suicide, and some of the family suspect a link to the old man's military service in Vietnam. However, this strand in the story simply peters out.

My own feeling is that Morton is too savvy a writer to have left these loose ends by mistake. And I guess all would have been revealed in a sequel that was to have been called *The Heroes of Muju*, in which Matt Johnson was to have represented the US in the Winter Olympics in Korea, while at the same time completing his own military service.

But it looks like we'll never know. *The Heroes of Muju* was scheduled for publication in 2007 but I think the publisher dropped it. I can't find it in any catalogue. Pity.

10.7 *Endless Winter — an Olympian's Journal (By Luke Bodensteiner)*

Posted on 5 January 2010

Endless Winter – an Olympian's Journal, by Luke Bodensteiner

Alta Press, Wisconsin 1994   ISBN 0-9643927-0-4

Endless Winter tells the story of an American cross-country skier's preparation for the 1994 Winter Olympics, which were held in Lillehammer, Norway. It spans the period from May 1993 to February 1994 and presents "A glimpse of [the author's] actions, thoughts, hopes, fears, successes and failures throughout the season".

The story opens: "This is it. Training begins today for the 1994 skiing season." At this time Bodensteiner is a final-year English student at the University of Utah in Salt Lake City. He had participated in the 1992 Olympics at Albertville where he had come 27th in his event. At Lillehammer he wants to do better and he dedicates the year towards that goal, living the life of a full-time ski racer.

In May he is training for 60 hours a month — mostly off-snow activities like running, roller-skiing and kayaking; but there is some spring skiing near Salt Lake and in Oregon. At about this time he leaves his student accommodation and effectively becomes homeless for the rest of the year. Dryland training in Utah gives way to summer skiing in Norway's Sognefjell, where he covers about 80km each day. The Norway trip culminates in a preview visit to Lillehammer, where the team goes up to Sjusjøen to check out the Olympic tracks.

Next comes a training camp in Michigan, then another spell in Utah. Then, in mid-October, he is off to Alaska for a month's training on snow. After that the racing season opens in the Alps and brings a rush of visits — to Austria's Tauplitz Alm, to Santa Caterina in Italy, to Davos in Switzerland and to Dobbiaco in the Dolomites.

On 1 January he flies again to Alaska, to take part in races that will determine team selection. Victory in two races assures his place in the Olympic team. By now the countdown to the Games is well under way and he is soon on his way to Lillehammer for his big moment.

And no, I'm not going to spoil the ending for you.

Endless Winter is a good story. It's well-enough told, and it is laced with interesting snippets of skiing lore, with gossipy suggestions of intrigue and infighting (and worse) in the racing establishment, and with delightfully barbed attacks on sports journalists, who are described variously as obnoxious, drunken and moronic.

The book was part of my holiday reading last week at Dalseter, a place not so far from Lillehammer. Temperatures were low for us — we skied on green wax every day bar one, when we used polar. The cold conditions brought clear skies that allowed us to stay out till four in the afternoon, which is not bad for late-December. But that still left plenty of après-ski hours for curling up with a book.

Endless Winter's diary format is just right for the casual kind of reading that you do on a ski holiday, when you are weary after the day's exertions and a more serious book would tip you over into sleep. And it seemed just right to be reading it at this time, when young ski racers round the world are getting ready for their own Olympic moments in Vancouver just a few weeks from now.

Sometimes Luke Bodensteiner is a little excitable as a writer and he can't always hold back from lofty observations like "In America there exists a strange dichotomy within the masses of people who work in and inhabit metropolitan areas".

But on the other hand he is capable of some truly stirring stuff. Consider this passage in praise of cross-country skiing:

"I love snow. I love mountain air and I love standing atop the world. I love being able to go pretty much anywhere I want to, using only my own powers. I love getting to places where other people don't venture. I love mountains and I love using my muscles. I love hanging myself out on the line and losing control so I can reel myself back in and know that I can control control. I love being a skier. I love being a skier who can go up and down and all-around — a skier who can ski it all."

That paragraph on its own justifies the £15 I paid for the book. And it came into my head a lot during the Dalseter week — on the long route back from Fefor where we had looked at photos of the snow-tractors that R.F. Scott took with him to the Antarctic; on the high circuit of Sprenpiggen, a route so good we did it twice; on the shady trails west of Espedalsvatn where the trees were draped with snow, and elk had stomped their hoof-prints into our nicely machined loipe.

10.8 Books about cross-country skiing — A list for World Book Day

Posted on 1 March 2012

It's World Book Day, and I've been doing my bit by compiling, on Amazon, a Listmania list of good books about cross-country skiing. Here it is, with my comments in quotation marks.

1. The First Crossing of Greenland, by Fridtjof Nansen

"Nansen's audacious east-west crossing of Greenland on skis in 1888. Did a lot to popularise skiing."

2. Journals: Captain Scott's Last Expedition (Oxford World's Classics), by Robert Falcon Scott

"Contrary to popular belief, Scott could ski — and was good at it. Shame about his expedition-management. (Snow-tractors!? In 1910!!??)"

3. The South Pole: The Norwegian Expedition in "The Fram", 1910-1912, by Roald Amundsen

"Unlike Scott, Amunsden was single-minded in his attempt on the Pole. The expedition relied on skis — and on dogs. Amundsen's drooling account of eating the dogs did little to help his popularity."

4. Cross-country Skiing, by Ned Gillette

"Popular and very readable 1970s how-to guidebook. Followed close after the success of US skier Bill Koch in the 1976 Winter Olympics."

5. Mountain Skiing, by Vic Bein

"Published in early 1980s. Was massively important in promoting mountain touring on Nordic equipment."

6. Serious Training for Endurance Athletes, by Rob Sleamaker

"Cross-country skiing is the endurance sport par excellence. Sleamaker's book has become a classic."

7. Long Distance: Testing the Limits of Body and Spirit in a Year of Living Strenuously, by Bill McKibben

"First published in 2000, this is the story of a thirty-something writer's attempt to live for a year the life of an elite athlete. (Sleamaker was his coach.) A practical and inspiring book."

8. A Medal of Honor: An Insider Unveils the Agony and the Ecstasy of the Olympic Dream, by John Morton

"One of the few novels about XC skiing written in English. It's a ripping yarn about elite biathlon. The author participated in six winter Olympics."

9. Momentum: Chasing the Olympic Dream, by Pete Vordenberg

"This is a brilliant book - "a memoir of a life in racing". Pete Vordenberg now coaches the US Team."

10. Tales of a Cross-Country Skier, by Guy Sheridan

"A Royal Marine's accounts of skiing in faraway places."

11. Cross-country Skiing, by Paddy Field & Tim Walker

"Noble attempt (in 1987) to popularise cross-country skiing to British readership."

12. Stride and Glide: A Manual of Cross-country Skiing and Nordic Walking, by Paddy Field & Stuart Montgomery

"Noble attempt (in 2006) to popularise cross-country skiing to British readership."

Okay, I need to ask you to forgive a bit of self-publicising in the last item…

10.9 *The Cross-Country Ski, Cook, Look & Pleasure Book (By Hal Painter)*

Posted on 15 January 2013

The Cross-Country Ski, Cook, Look & Pleasure Book, by Hal Painter

Wilderness Press, Berkeley 1973

Recently we mentioned on *XCuk's* Facebook site that Parks Canada was to stop grooming ski trails in national parks. The argument was familiar: costs were high, funds were scarce and the federal government had cut the budget.

But it was a controversial decision, especially in Saskatchewan where skiers organised an online petition. In just a few days they had 2500 signatories. On the face of it, they had an excellent case. Cross-country skiing is a healthy form of exercise, and at a time of growing obesity and lifestyle-related illness the State should be encouraging participation, not preventing it.

Yet for me it jarred. For aren't we the folk who practise the "go-anywhere" form of skiing, the form that allows us to explore at will, to make our own trails through the virgin powder? No one was proposing to close these Canadian parks. Free access would continue. But the protesters seemed to be saying, *You can't expect us to ski in there. The tracks are all covered in snow!*

Now I have to be careful when I start thinking like this, or I'll awaken one of my bonnet-bees. The one that buzzes on about how XC skiing has become too performance-based, too reliant on manicured surfaces and over-specified kit, too obsessed with damn-fool stunts — like up-on-the-toenails-double-poling and V57 skating — that don't have the slightest utility on proper snow. And don't get me started about short-radius Telemarks on fat skis or I'll fetch up in a 150 beats per minute rant about how we've evolved our sport to the point where it's lost all functionality. *Cross-country* skiing? Hah! Take away the grooming machine and we simply can't move!! Hah!!

At such times I'm glad to have a copy of Hal Painter's book. As befits a volume called *The Cross-Country Ski, Cook, Look & Pleasure Book — and welcome to the Alice in snowpeople land,* it always has a calming effect.

Published in 1973 it is an eccentric attempt by an unreconstructed hippy to write a *How-to* book that doesn't forget the question *Why*. And his answer to that question has everything to do with fun and nature and discovery — and nothing at all to do with performance.

"On my fortieth birthday," Painter writes, "I bought a fancy pair of skis for forty-six dollars and eighty-one cents and said, The hell with it: my feet are trying to tell me something. I followed to see where they were going … I made friends with a bearded troll, who's pushing fifty as easily as younger men push wheelbarrows full of goose down."

The troll is Rune, a Swede, whose instructional method is technically minimalist. "Ski like cat, slow and easy, slow and easy. Relax. Be graceful like the cat. Smart like the cat, too. You go all day through the woods, enjoy it, have fun". Yet the method is effective and Painter gets good enough to go on long ski treks in Yosemite. Over time he picks up enough lore and wisdom to feel he can write a book.

But just as he's getting into his writing stride, there comes a chapter based on a letter from "Alice". Perhaps Alice is the naked young woman on the fly-leaf, standing in a vegetable garden alongside a seated and equally naked companion whose own modesty is assured by the live chicken nestling on his lap — but this is not made clear. In winter Alice lives in an igloo (with Stanley) and puzzles over how to make yogurt in that environment. Bean sprouts are okay, you just bag them up and take them into your sleeping bag. But with yogurt that might not work. They have a Chinese friend, Harry, who made his own skis from chop-suey crates. Under the base tar you can read *Golden Junk Brand Shrimp Chips*. Harry is a cook and has a deep scorn for the cookbooks that Alice shows him. "Chinese man no learn to cook from cookbook, he go to kitchen and talk to Chinese cook."

It needs to be said that, even when Painter does get into his stride, he is capable of writing hundred-carat twaddle. Several entire chapters are silly and totally without value: on the Zen of skiing, on making skis from ferrocement, on ski waxing and on using klister. And even in the better stuff he is always ready to slip into a childish whimsy that is probably hilarious if you are smoking herby cigarettes but isn't if you're not.

Yet you might just forgive him when you read his account of the 1960s resurgence of cross-country skiing, which he sees as a reaction against downhill skiing. Not just a rejection of the commercial over-development of the resorts, but a rebellion against Pavlovian instructors focussed on ensuring uniformity in the conveyor belt world of piste skiing. "The sound of the ski coach's sternest admonishment was heard round the world: keep the skis together, make a straight and narrow track. Violators were perfunctorily dismissed; nonconformists need not reapply."

By contrast, cross-country skiing promised "fun and games, free form and *élan vital*" and presently "a ragamuffin army mounted on hickory staves … declared an open war of rebellion."

When such polemics threaten to get a little heavy, Alice's letters prove their worth as a mood-lightening device. But even "she" manages to include jokey comments about over-instructing and about commercialisation — "slicky ads with pictures of epoxy chicks in seventy-five-dollar knickers". (There is a really funny Alice chapter about how she and Stanley have learned to enjoy sex in the snow. Be warned, it's explicit stuff.)

The chapter *Keeping in Shape Like the Boiled Asparagus* is a wonderful mickey-take of competitive skiing. "Swedish scientists, after many tests and exhaustive conferences, have decided beyond doubt that cross-country can be the most strenuous sport known to man." Painter clearly doesn't think this is a good thing. "A muscular ordeal on skis is just plain dumb if body and head suffer for it," he suggests, and laments that racers are discovering in XC "one more squeaky battlefield of male aggressions."

Like the chapter on pushy, up-selling salespeople, it's good knockabout stuff.

After reading the book I'm no less uneasy about where our sport is going. But, by hokey, I'm chilled. Hey, if people feel the need to slog round rollerski tracks double-poling on their toenails — well, man, that's cool with me. And if they insist on using skis too thin to keep them out of the drift, that's just dandy. It keeps the mountains quieter, I say, able now to smile at the memory of the instructor who recently despaired of my poor weight transfer. Too much touring, he said, generously expanding my list of oxymorons. Grateful to you, buddy.

ABOUT THE AUTHOR

After many years of mountaineering in his native Scotland, Stuart Montgomery worked as a leader of overseas walking and cross-country skiing groups for a company called Waymark Holidays. In 1990 he accepted the offer of an "office job" with Waymark and eventually became its Managing Director.

From 2005 to 2014 he was a director of *XCuk*, a travel company that organised holidays for cross-country skiers.

Other entries in his CV include social researcher and university lecturer (in Scotland), furnace operator (in Norway), fitness instructor and postman. He has held instructor qualifications in Nordic skiing, Nordic walking and mountain navigation and is a qualified personal trainer.

He has also written (with Paddy Field) *Stride and Glide: A Manual of Cross-Country Skiing and Nordic Walking*.

In 2015 he published *The Red Mitten*, a novel based on ski-touring and set mainly in Norway.

Printed in Great Britain
by Amazon